DOUBLE
YOUR INCOME
WITH
NETWORK
MARKETING

DOUBLE
YOUR INCOME

WITH

NETWORK
MARKETING

CREATE **FINANCIAL SECURITY**
IN JUST MINUTES A DAY . . .
WITHOUT QUITTING YOUR JOB

TY TRIBBLE

WILEY

John Wiley & Sons, Inc.

Published by John Wiley & Sons, Inc., Hoboken, New Jersey.
Published simultaneously in Canada.

For general information on our other products and services or for technical support, please contact our Customer Care Department within the United States at (800) 762-2974, outside the United States at (317) 572-3993 or fax (317) 572-4002.

Wiley publishes in a variety of print and electronic formats and by print-on-demand. Some material included with standard print versions of this book may not be included in e-books or in print-on-demand. If this book refers to media such as a CD or DVD that is not included in the version you purchased, you may download this material at http://booksupport.wiley.com. For more information about Wiley products, visit www.wiley.com.

Library of Congress Cataloging-in-Publication Data:

Tribble, Ty, 1970–
    Double your income with network marketing : create financial security in just minutes
a day . . . without quitting your job / Ty Tribble.
        pages. cm.
    Includes index.
    ISBN: 978-1-118-12197-9 (pbk)
    ISBN: 978-1-118-22465-6 (ebk)
    ISBN: 978-1-118-23810-3 (ebk)
    ISBN: 978-1-118-26278-8 (ebk)
        1. Multilevel marketing. 2. Direct marketing. I. Title.
    HF5415.126.T75 2012
    658.8'72—dc23   2011046344

Printed in the United States of America
10 9 8 7 6 5 4 3 2 1

Contents

Preface

Double Your Income

TAHITIAN BEER IN hand, relaxing on the beach at an exclusive resort in Bora Bora with a dozen great friends, I pulled out my phone to check my e-mail.

"Congratulations, Ty, your $25,000 Fast Track check is being mailed today."

Then I realized that the $25,000 check was only part of my income for the month, and here I was taking eight days off at one of the most exclusive resorts in the world.

My home for the week was a 1,100-square-foot bungalow sitting over crystal clear turquoise water. I calculated that the bungalow was roughly 200 square feet bigger than the first home my wife and I owned as newlyweds.

Apparently 85-degree weather makes me want to do math because while sitting under the umbrella, gazing across the bluest water I have ever seen, I also calculated that I had worked somewhere in the neighborhood of 40 hours in the previous month. Not 40 hours per week, but 40 hours total for the month.

I was working less but getting paid more in the misunder-stood industry of network marketing.

But it wasn't always like that.

Time seemed to stop for a moment as I reflected on my early struggles in the network marketing industry. My biggest check in my first five years was $1,200, and I spent more than $1,000 that month on seminars and training, leaving me a net, grand total of $200 in my very best month.

I started to think about what separated our success from those who tried and failed, and I realized that it really came down to one thing.

We never gave up.

I believe that you already possess the talent that it takes to double your income in the next 24 months, and this book will provide you with the strategy and techniques you'll need.

You will need to bring focus, ambition, and a willingness to learn.

There will be times when you feel like you are getting nowhere, fast.

Robert Kiyosaki said, ". . . what makes people rich is not the money. What makes people rich are skills."

If you develop (and apply) the right skills, the money will come.

My friend and mentor, Bo Short, puts it this way: "It's not just doing the right things; it's doing enough of the right things that will bring you success."

There is an old question/riddle that helps illustrate this point: Would you rather have a million dollars in cash or a penny doubled every day for 30 days?

Of course, most people will think that this must be a trick question and lean toward the penny doubled, but at the same time, they salivate over the million dollars in cash.

On day 7, the guy who took the million dollars in cash is probably driving around town in his new Ferrari, whereas the "penny-doubled" guy has a whopping 64 cents in his pocket.

Day 14, penny-doubled guy has $81.92. He might be able to buy dinner and a movie if he scrimps on the dinner and skips the popcorn at the movie theater. Meanwhile, "million-in-cash" guy is inviting people over to his new home for a hot tub party.

Day 21 comes and penny-doubled guy looks like an idiot because he has only $10,485.76. At this point we are about 75 percent of the way to the finish line and this guy has $989,000.00 less than the million-in-cash guy. Ouch.

But something crazy happens on day 28. Penny-doubled guy now has $1,342,177.28, passing million-in-cash guy for the first time.

On day 30, million-in-cash guy is crying because penny-doubled guy now has more than $5 million, five times the million dollars he took.

The riddle is a lesson in patience and perseverance.

Six months into starting his business, *Beach Money* author Jordan Adler was making less than $100 per month.

A full two years into launching, Adler was making $1,350 a month; yet a year later he passed $20,000 per month.

Today, Adler earns in excess of $1 million a year, all while taking more than 10 weeks off to vacation in Europe and the Caribbean and spend time on his personal development.

Jordan Adler and I are with different companies, but our stories are very similar.

We struggled but never quit.

There was one thing that kept us both going: the amazing power of having a dream.

Acknowledgments

I WOULD LIKE to thank my coach, mentor, and friend, Bo Short, for believing in me. Bo's guidance and leadership have been invaluable to my family and me.

I want to thank my mom, Clydette, for her encouragement and dedication.

To my dads Brian Kuehn and Dr. Richard Ewing, thank you for being incredible examples for me to follow; and to my other mom, René Ewing, your love and support has been a wonderful blessing that I would not know how to live without.

Finally I wish to thank my wife Richelle and our two children, Emma and Tyler. I tend to get the applause when I stand onstage and speak, yet they are the real stars.

PART

I

Your Transformation Starts Here

1

Your Dreams and Goals

WHEN I WAS in kindergarten, I spent a lot of time playing with Hot Wheels and Matchbox cars. My memory of playing with my buddies Johnny and Tyler are vivid, even today, 35 years later.

Every day started out the same; we would take out our favorite cars and park them in the garage that we had built into the side of our rockery. The driveway up to our makeshift mansion of sticks and rocks was long, and Johnny, Tyler, and I dreamed of being rich. I'm not sure we knew what a millionaire was at that age, but in our little Matchbox dream, we were wealthy.

At least eight cars would park in our driveway each day. At any time you might find a black 1957 Chevy with red, yellow, and orange fire flames on the sides, the Scooby Doo Mystery Machine, a convertible red 1974 Corvette Stingray, a lime green dune buggy, a silver Porsche 917 Grand Prix, a blue Ferrari race car, a tank, and an ambulance.

We would spend hours pretending to be the guy who lived in the mansion on the hill and drove the coolest cars that money could buy. Johnny, Tyler, and I dreamed big. When we would see a cool car, driving down the street, we would always dream of having one ourselves one day.

Then at some point in our lives, we are all told to stop dreaming, be more realistic and get reasonable with our goals in life. It's an easy trap to fall into. We often get so caught up in the day-to-day life of commuting to work, focusing on our jobs, and chauffeuring the kids from school to sports and other activities that we lose sight of what is actually possible.

I understand that it would be completely unrealistic to believe that a person could work 40 hours in a month and get paid 10 times more than he or she made at a job working more than 240 hours per month. But, that is exactly what happened to me.

Dreams and goals help you drive past the little challenges that happen and allow you to focus on where you are going in the long run. Another way to put it is if you are looking down at the ground while you are walking, you are likely to run into something (like a signpost). If you look forward, you will better navigate around the signpost. Remember that the signpost (or challenge) did not disappear, you simply moved past it on your way to your destination.

The first step to building a business is to understand why you are building it in the first place.

Another example I like to talk about with our team is building a boat. There are some things that you need in order to build a boat: plans, materials, tools, and so on. But if you want to motivate someone (including yourself) to build a boat, you don't talk about the plans or materials. Talk about what it will feel like when the warm wind hits your face as you sail across crystal blue water. Talk about what the sunset looks like in Tahiti.

Jonas Salk said, "There is hope in dreams, imagination, and in the courage of those who wish to make those dreams a reality."

This book will supply you with a blueprint for building a six-figure income, but you must supply the dream, imagination, and courage that will allow you to overlook the daily challenges of life in order to focus on the bigger picture.

Nearly every significant accomplishment in the world started with a dream that was larger than any set backs the world could bring against it.

Bob Parsons, the chief executive officer (CEO) of GoDaddy .com, put it this way: "What kept me going through the hard times was the vision I kept in my mind's eye and seldom let go of. This vision always dealt with the rewards of succeeding.

While I thought often and long about what I needed to do to succeed, the vision that kept me going had nothing to do with the mechanics of success."

I know that some of you (with the same personality type as mine) are chomping at the bit, wondering when I am going to get to the techniques, strategies, and blueprints to earn a six-figure income. I understand exactly how you feel, but you must realize that having a clear vision of what it will be like when you succeed is step one to attaining the success you are looking for.

I like to approach dreams and goals a little differently than you might expect.

Grab a pen and a fresh notebook and quickly write down four things that you would like to accomplish in the following eight areas (don't spend a ton of time on this right now, just write down what first comes to mind):

1. Physical health/fitness
2. Financial
3. Career/profession
4. Family life
5. Personal development/education
6. Spiritual
7. Friendships
8. Travel

This exercise will help you clarify what is most important to you and how these things are interconnected.

Once you have the four things that you would like to accomplish in all eight areas, fill out the bracket (see Figure 1.1) with the information.

Next, run your own mini-final four tournament to determine what is most important to you. As you go through this

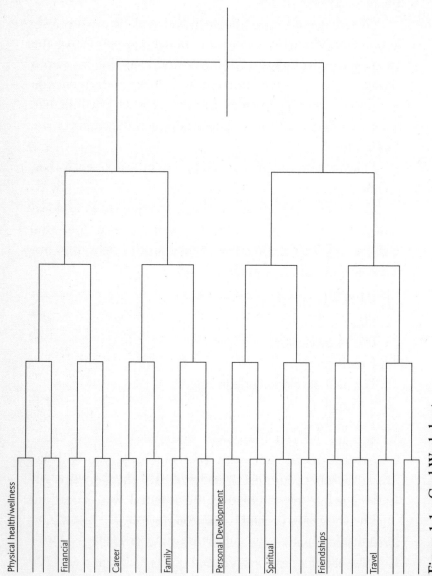

Physical health/wellness

Financial

Career

Family

Personal Development

Spiritual

Friendships

Travel

Figure 1.1 Goal Worksheet

exercise, you will find that in many areas, accomplishing one thing would automatically lead to accomplishing several other things on your list.

For example, if one of your travel goals is to spend five weeks traveling and experiencing the culture of Europe, this might be accomplished as a by-product of hitting a particular career or financial goal.

By the time you get to the end of your bracket, you will have a pretty good picture of your dreams and goals.

Think about what is most important to you and what you really want to accomplish in your life. The reason I suggested that you start with a fresh notebook is because your next step is to find pictures that represent those important dreams. Create a page in the notebook that is specific to the most important dreams and goals and tape in the pictures that best represent what you are looking for in life.

This notebook is your lifeline, your instant pick-me-up. Whenever you feel down, whenever you feel like things are not going your way, you refer back to your notebook for an injection of "the reason why you are taking the steps to build a better life." No matter how difficult things get or how many roadblocks you run into, the things in your notebook will always be worth the effort it takes to push through, face the challenges, and work toward your end goals.

As you spend time with your notebook, you will find that sometimes your dreams and goals will change; many will evolve, and a few might even be replaced with something that feels more important. Your notebook should be a living, breathing document, not something static that sits in a drawer.

No matter what your dream, big or small, make sure that it moves you. Your dream should stir something in your gut. W. Clement Stone said, "When you discover your mission, you will feel its demand. It will fill you with enthusiasm and a burning desire to get to work on it."

Those who accomplish great things in their life always have struggles. They all must deal with naysayers and critics who do not share their belief and dream. Your dream notebook will provide a visual glimpse into your heart. Think of the notebook as a bird's eye view into the person you want to become.

Here's how Apple cofounder, Steve Jobs put it:

> Your time is limited, so don't waste it living someone else's life. Don't be trapped by dogma—which is living with the results of other people's thinking. Don't let the noise of others' opinions drown out your own inner voice. And most important, have the courage to follow your heart and intuition. They somehow already know what you truly want to become. Everything else is secondary.

By choosing to limit the noise of others and follow his heart, Steve Jobs made a massive impact on the way people interact with technology.

It was Jobs' vision of what the future could look like that set him apart. That vision and an almost stubborn devotion to getting things right reminds me of one of my friends, Marcia Norfleet.

Marcia Norfleet is an amazing example of a woman on a mission, driven to find a way to build financial security for her family in her mid-40s. Her dream to become financially independent has been accomplished through the network marketing industry. I had a chance to sit down with Marcia and ask her about her experience and success with the industry:

Ty Tribble: You achieved a high level of success in a short time with your company. What is your secret?

Marcia Norfleet: Everything that I'm sharing here comes as a result of my attendance at the school of hard knocks on my part. My desire in sharing this information is for others to shorten their learning curve, to come out of the gate with knowledge of how to succeed in the marketplace utilizing the most powerful business model ever devised—network marketing. I believe that network marketing is poised to become the business model of choice in getting goods and services around the globe. Individuals who have the discipline to learn how to build a team and lead a team will be global leaders and global earners. I believe the industry is on the verge of an explosion and I celebrate you for being a student of the industry.

When I learned about the business model, I quickly grasped the concept of time leveraging and residual income; however, I did not understand how to channel my enthusiasm. I believed that everyone would share my beliefs, and if they did not jump at the chance to join me, I was shocked, and unfortunately I thought I needed to talk more and more and faster and faster and then I would say something to bring them around. The more I talked, the more frustrated the person became with me and with the industry. What I am sharing now comes from my continuation and determination to win in the industry and from allowing others to mentor, coach, and train me.

First and foremost, a person who begins a business is encouraged to find a mentor. It's interesting to me that people come out of the woodwork to give advice to a person who starts a network marketing business. Most of the advice comes from well-meaning people who have never built a successful business in the industry, but they give all kinds of negative advice. I encourage you to not take advice from someone who has not been successful in the industry. A mentor will guide you and advise you and keep you focused and on track.

My next success tip centers around self-belief. When a person decides to build a new business, whether traditional business or in direct sales, self-belief is an internal compass. I have learned that we will never accomplish what we wish for or think about; we will accomplish only what we can envision. I had to learn to close my eyes and see a huge room full of people who have locked arms and are sharing the power of time leveraging, offering right-now income and long-term residual income with me. I have heard it said that the world steps out of the way for a person who knows where he or she is going. I'd like to add that individuals will join you only when you exhibit confidence in where you are going and in your ability to take them with you. I caution here: Individuals are not attracted to self-centered people who boast about what they have done and what they are going to do; they are attracted to what can be done with and for them. Servant leadership is a good description of the type of leadership that I have adopted. The mind-set of a servant leader is one of giving back more than they take from within the marketplace. Life gives each of us exactly what we ask for and bargain for. Servant leaders ask, "Who can I serve? Who will walk with me as we impact lives utilizing the business model of direct sales?"

A third determining factor of my success was learning to ask questions instead of making statements. I believe that asking is endearing and telling is repelling. Have you heard it said that no one likes to be sold, but everyone likes to buy? No one likes to be told, but most everyone likes to be asked, specifically about what he or she wants out of life. Learn to ask questions and answer your prospects' questions with a question.

Next, be mindful that with the first word from your mouth with a prospect, you are training that person on how you conduct business and what it will be like to be in business with you. You are representing yourself first and foremost, your company of choice next. Your prospects buy into you prior to even considering the company you represent.

Spend at least 20 to 30 minutes daily reading from experts about leadership. Everything rises and falls on leadership. Mental preparation for your day is important; I choose to read in the morning.

Lastly, when you know where you are going and what you are going to accomplish, your self-image is not directly impacted by a person's individual decision to join you in your business or not. The potential business partner feels your confidence, but they do not feel that you need them for fulfillment. This mind-set is very powerful and compelling. I made a decision about how I want to treat my prospects that has served very well: Every person who I introduce to my business, no matter how that person responds to me and my business, will leave my presence feeling better about himself or herself.

Ty Tribble: With that mind-set, what attracted you to your current company?

Marcia Norfleet: Everyone works for one thing, pretty much—money! The company I represent lays out a six-figure income in 15 months, with two luxury trips and a car payment. Most important, the pathway to $100,000 is doable for anyone, even a person who has never been involved in the industry, not just for the top producers. We have individuals earning significantly who had no prior industry experience. That is huge for me.

The company also is stable; it has been in business for 55 years and is the number-one natural nutrition company in America. I also belong to a leadership group that conducted an extensive search to find the best opportunity, and we are all in agreement that we are building with the best company, products, and compensation plan. The leadership of the company and the leadership of our group are in step; our visions are to impact millions globally with healthy products and finances.

Ty Tribble: Has social media made an impact on your business?

Marcia Norfleet: Social media has greatly impacted my ability to let people know that I am in the business of coaching others to start their own businesses. Facebook is my favorite social media tool; it is easy and does not take much time. Most of my posts are about food, family, and fun; then I post requests such as, "I am looking to partner with two to three people who will commit to earning six figures in the next 15 months with a couple of luxury trips, please inbox me to learn more." When people answer me, I pick up the phone and call them and ask them, "What's got you looking around?" Then we set an appointment if they live near me; if not, they are directed to our leadership website to watch a webinar explaining the business opportunity. It is refreshing when people come to you because they are looking. Please note, I still keep a list of people whom I call and invite to gather information about a project I am bringing into the area. I do not rely totally on social media.

Ty Tribble: You are known for your ability to "ask for the business." Talk about the questions you ask a potential business partner at the end of a meeting.

Marcia Norfleet: Ending a meeting and conducting what I call discovery is so much fun for me; however, without the beginning questions it is difficult to accomplish.

When a person has agreed to sit down with you, there are three questions that are powerful and will give you insight as to how you can sponsor your prospect. These came from my mentors and our leadership group. In this business, the best copycat wins!

Let's use "John" as an example. Start by saying, "John, I'm going to ask you a few hypothetical questions." And then proceed:

1. "John, if what I am about to show you works for you now, what kind of income will you be looking for? A few hundred monthly, replacement income, or dramatic income?" Then close your mouth and let John answer; he may speak for several minutes—listen to him.

2. "John, if what I'm about to show you could get you _____(fill in with John's answer), what will that change in your life?" Again, no talking; listen.

3. "John, if this could get you _____(John's answer from question 2), could you carve some time out of an already busy schedule to make it happen?" Again, listen; let John talk. And notice that you didn't say how much time. Even if John asks, "How much time?" don't answer; say simply, "John, that will be up to you."

I get very excited about what these questions do for prospects. Remember, asking is endearing. The first question opens the person's window of possibility, and he or she sits taller because you just indicated that what you're about to show is significant. The second question tells you what the prospect wants to change and how you can spon-sor him or her. The third question eliminates the most utilized objection—time. While the prospect's curiosity is at a heightened state, you hear a commitment that the person can carve out the time.

Show your plan, keep it under 30 minutes, and then look up and say, "John, what do you find most intriguing about the information you just gathered?" We don't say, "What I just told you . . ." because telling is repelling. How you use your words is very important.

John will tell you exactly what his interest is, and he will do it with total ease and openness. If his interest is in the product only, you can set him up as a customer and ask for referrals. If he gives my favorite answer, one that I anticipate with every meeting—"Everything," meaning business model and products—I ask, "What questions can I answer for you about getting started?" Again, I lead John where I want him to go. If he has no questions or when we are done, I ask, "So, John, do you see yourself starting your own business and partnering with us to begin earning income right away?" As I speak, I slide an application and pen over to him and I stop talking. John will either pick up the pen and begin writing or ask me another question. If he is not prepared to get started today, I will find out what his due diligence consists of and ask for the follow-up meeting the next day. If he cannot meet then, I ask for the day after that. I leave the meeting with a new distributor or a clear understanding of how he will make his decision and what, if any, his obstacles are. Only then do I know how to open the follow-up meeting.

Ty Tribble: What characteristics do you look for in a potential business partner?

Marcia Norfleet: Integrity, positive energy, character, influence, and intention are my top five criteria when I am expanding my list of contacts. To expand my list, I use social media and referrals. Referrals are a powerful way to quickly expand a prospect list.

My initial instincts were to "prequalify" individuals. Some appeared to be too successful; others, not successful enough. I searched out people who fell in the middle, if you will. That was a mistake. I learned not to make decisions for others. I learned to simply ask, "Are you open to gathering information about a project I am bringing into the area?" or "Do you know of someone who might be interested in gathering information about partnering with me to earn six figures in 15 months with a couple of luxury trips and a car payment?"

Ty Tribble: What do you think holds some people back from looking at network marketing as a viable business?

Marcia Norfleet: My initial response to this question is the typical stereotype that is given to individuals who participate in the industry. The industry has attracted some bad actors in the past as "get-rich-quick" promises flowed quite freely. Nothing is free. The price of winning in network marketing is personal growth, development of your leadership skills and the leadership skills of those around you, and willingness to serve others. One of my passions for the industry is to be one of the individuals who is responsible for changing the opinion of the industry by working and living a life of excellence. The reputation of the industry will change as we continue to attract and recruit individuals with character, integrity, influence, intention, and positive energy. I am already seeing a positive shift within the leadership group that I belong to and the company we choose to represent.

Ty Tribble: What are some of the rewards that you have been able to participate in as a result of network marketing?

Marcia Norfleet: The biggest reward that I see from the industry is the personal growth that I am experiencing. Every area of my life is richer and more fulfilling because I am serving in an industry that I believe will change millions of lives around the globe. Keeping the vision of the future of the industry in my mind daily, I am empowered to share what I am doing with others in such a way that people respond positively.

On a more personal level, I own my time again. I determine each day how I utilize the day, whom I work with, and how much I accomplish. I don't ask permission to take off work for family outings any longer. I spend my time working with like-minded individuals who are goal-oriented and who give back in a big way. My family has been able to travel to exotic locations that I would have never dreamed of prior to my introduction to the industry. My children are very proud of what I am doing, and they know that with every call I make, every appointment and every follow-up, I am securing our financial future. I am planning to leave my children a financial heritage, one that will continue giving long after my work here on earth is completed.

2

The Social Marketing Revolution

ACCORDING TO KELLER Fay at the WOMMA Presentation in 2010, the average consumer mentions specific brands more than 90 times per week in conversations with friends, family, and coworkers. And unless you are already involved in the network marketing industry, there is little likelihood that any of those companies sent you a thank-you check last week.

As of this writing, Facebook has grown to more than 800 million active users without ever doing a television commercial. How many times have you heard, "Are you on Facebook? Oh my gosh, you have to get on Facebook." Basically, we are all doing Facebook's advertising for them, and the investors love us.

It's the 800 million Facebook users who invited their friends to participate that has created one of the most valuable companies in the world, yet we are unable to participate in any of the financial value.

We continuously create value in the marketplace for companies that we like when we share our product experiences with friends and family members, and our voice can be greatly amplified through social media.

Let's say that you're out with a couple of your friends at a local sports bar and decide to have someone take a picture of you and your buddies. You hand over your phone, and the picture is taken. One of your friends suggests that you upload the picture to Facebook.

So you post the picture to Facebook and write a short caption: "Bryan, Ernie, and I are hanging out at Jersey's Sports Bar. The nachos were awesome and the beer is ice cold. Gotta love it. Go Seahawks." Of course, Facebook is smart and the site suggests the last names of your friends as you are typing, so they are now "tagged" on the picture.

Here's where it gets fun. The average Facebook user has 130 friends. So in about two minutes, you just told 390 people (the collective number of Facebook friends of you and your pals) about the nachos and beer at Jersey's Sports bar.

Now think about these phenomena as an opportunity—the opportunity to communicate a message about products that you love from a company that will pay you to spread the word.

Collectively, we spent the past few years building value for Facebook, but at the same time, we created our own living and breathing network that lives within the Facebook technology.

In *The Business School for People Who Like Helping People*, author Robert Kiyosaki states, "The richest people in the world build networks. Everyone else is trained to look for work." The good news is that without even really knowing it, many of us have been busy building a network on Facebook.

As a network marketer back in the 1990s, I was basically taught to go meet people at the mall or hang out in the business books section of the local bookstore to find prospects for my business. Not only can this type of cold networking make you feel like a stalker (like I did), but it can be a challenge for many people. I believe that the teaching of these techniques is one of the main reasons why so many people got started in the industry but chose to quit shortly thereafter.

Technology can be very uncomfortable for many people, including those network marketing leaders who built their business in the 1980s. Rather than embrace the new technology and merge the best technological breakthroughs with the tried-and-true methods of personal connections and relationship building, many of these leaders shunned technology. Some of them even bragged about not being able to check their e-mail.

Technology can be a scary thing, especially for those of us born before 1990. I sometimes use an example of what it would feel like if you were an immigrant in a country where you didn't speak the language. That is how many people feel about technology. At the same time, we talk about the younger generation that seems to automatically "get it" when it comes to smartphones, social media, and touch-screen computers. Of course they get it! The younger generations are "natives" in the technology environment. They speak the language. They have never lived in a home without a computer.

You might find this generation (Generation Z or The Internet Generation) watching TV while texting a friend and posting on Facebook. For the natives, it would be no different than someone from Generation X reading the newspaper while eating a sandwich.

The ability to quickly and easily communicate an idea in a rapid fashion has pushed the network marketing industry into what I consider revolutionary territory.

According to John David Mann in the book *It's Time for Network Marketing*, some 70,000 people who are not currently involved in the network marketing industry will be involved at this time tomorrow.

The industry of direct selling, which encompasses network marketing as well as more traditional companies such as Tupperware, is currently a $114 billion worldwide industry.

The Social Marketing Revolution is a new way to build a business with a proven business model that has existed for more than 50 years.

Network marketing leader Aspen Emry and her husband Brent have four children under the age of nine yet still run a very successful traditional business in addition to their large network marketing organization. I had the opportunity to ask

Aspen a handful of questions that might give you some insight into what it takes to be successful in the network marketing industry:

Ty Tribble: You have four children under age nine. How do you balance being a mom and wife with a multimillion-dollar business?

Aspen Emry: The key to balancing this incredible business is using a calendar and being extremely diligent about making sure the family's important events are written on it before business fills in some of the gaps. By marking out clear hours each week for business, we can eliminate having to choose between family time and business time. Another very important factor in making it work is being sure that the time I dedicate to my business is spent on the activities that are income producing or high-pay-off activities. When you are in a position of balancing life and a family, you quickly learn which activities are worth making time for and which ones aren't helping you reach your goals.

Ty Tribble: You have attracted what I consider to be major league talent to your team from all walks of life, including motivational speakers, athletes, and business owners. What attracts already successful people to the industry?

Aspen Emry: Successful people already understand the benefits of working smarter not harder, and they have a keen eye for opportunities that allow them to leverage their time while earning residual income. When the right opportunity comes along and is presented in a concise, confident, and professional way, they are able to see how it will add value to their life and money in the bank. They understand the importance, especially in this economy, of having multiple streams of income.

Ty Tribble: Facebook seems to be a great tool for you in attracting people to your business. What works well for you, and what have you tried that didn't quite work?

Aspen Emry: Facebook has been an incredible tool to attract people both to the products and to the business. I've found that limiting the amount of posts about my company, business, and products (maybe 1 out of 10 to 15 posts are about business) keeps people tuned in to my life and not turned off to my business. When they are bombarded, they start to tune it out. By mentioning a result of a product I'm trying, pictures of a check I've earned, or mentioning a free trip we're taking because of our business, people are drawn to what it's all about because they see it's *real* and not hype at all.

What I've seen that clearly does not work (at least within our group) is any sort of "mass" Facebook message. This business must be heart-to-heart and belly-to-belly even when using Facebook. There needs to be a personal touch when reaching out through social media.

Ty Tribble: Your team loves to have fun. Talk about how relationships and fun events impact your business.

Aspen Emry: Honestly, I would have to say that the relationship part of this business is my number-one success tool. Of course there are many things that help, but by being genuine with people, I've come further than I ever thought possible. My team and my relationships with them are what keep us going through the peaks and valleys of this business. We work hard, but we make time to play hard as well. We have family get-togethers with our teammates, go to dinner and movies, and keep in touch about life on a regular basis. They are so much more than an ID number or a volume amount. Anyone can sponsor someone into the business, but it's keeping that person in, helping him or her grow as a leader, and providing mentoring that is going to turn your business into a large stream of residual income for generations to come.

Ty Tribble: Is there a network marketing product that has made an impact on your life?

Aspen Emry: Cinch weight-loss products by Shaklee. I would say specifically the meal and snack bars. After four kids all born in a five-year time span, weight was a constant battle. Being on the run and too busy was my excuse for about three years and I found myself yo-yo dieting. Within five months of starting on the Cinch program, I was 60 pounds down. Now *that* is an impact on my life!

Ty Tribble: What are your long-term goals for your business?

Aspen Emry: I want a business that is strong, stable, and generational. We are building a legacy that will be passed down to our children and grandchildren.

Ty Tribble: Tell us about some of the rewards you have experienced or will experience in the next 12 months.

Aspen Emry: We have received thousands of dollars in incredible overrides and bonuses. We've taken a free trip to San Francisco with the "royal treatment," and we are traveling to the Bahamas with our whole family for free! This next 12 months will be even more incredible. We'll be seeing our teammate earn thousands more dollars in bonuses as well as ourselves and will be taking *two* free *international* trips this year. No other career path can offer us the freedom, flexibility, and lifestyle that we have here.

3

Choosing the Right Company

ONE OF THE biggest problems associated with the industry of network marketing is that most people do very little research when it comes to the company they sign on with. And even if you ultimately do your research, traditional business criteria may not be applicable to finding the right network marketing company for you.

As you read though the guidelines and suggestions that I provide in this chapter, you may come to the conclusion that I'm biased. My answer to that allegation is that *of course I am biased*. I have spent more than 20 years in the industry of network marketing, and I have seen what works and what doesn't work. Over the years, I have paid close attention to what works for the newest person.

If you are currently involved with a certain type of company and what I say next goes against what you are being told, I would ask you to consider how long you have been with the company and how much you are currently making in bonus money each month. Before you go on the attack, be sure that you are having the success you expected. There are always exceptions to the rules.

In the past year, I had the opportunity to choose a new company for my team and myself, and I (along with a group of leaders) created a list of criteria that we used to find the best long-term fit for our team.

- **Security:** Few network marketers think about security when they go into business. In most cases, the sales pitch talks about the latest and greatest ground floor deal. I used to be one of those people who thought that the ground floor was the place to be.

The problem with the ground floor opportunity is that very few of them will last. There is no denying that timing is important when choosing an opportunity, but there can be great timing with companies that are not likely going out of business within the next 12 months.

One of the main attractions to network marketing is the opportunity to earn residual income, but income quickly becomes not so residual when a company goes out of business or changes its business model.

Some suggest that you make sure that the company has been in business for at least five years, but five years isn't a very long time. I'd probably go a step further and suggest that the company be in business for at least 10 years. You can negotiate this point, but you will also be negotiating your ability to eventually step back from the day-to-day work and enjoy the rewards of a true residual income.

- **Products:** This is an area where I will likely take some heat from people who are currently involved with particular companies. Just about every company I have been exposed to will claim that they have the best products. The truth of the matter is that they can't all be the best.

When it comes to choosing the right product, the first thing that I think about is finding a product that will make an impact on people's lives.

An example might be the scientifically proven weight loss system by Shaklee, called Cinch, or a greeting card that can be sent from your computer at about one-third the price of a card found in stores like the Send Out Cards product.

One of the fastest ways to gain customers for your business is to be able to offer a real testimonial about the impact of a product. If you lose 20 pounds on the Cinch Weight Loss Challenge, people will ask you how you did it; through the process of telling them what you did, you will gain customers.

I prefer to stay away from network marketing companies touting services such as phone-related services and electricity. People are often too reluctant to change from their current service to something they don't have confidence in. Avoid competing with companies such as Verizon, Comcast, and AT&T, or your local powerful electric company.

In addition, I suggest that you avoid the increasing number of network marketing companies that are cropping up in the travel industry. Beware of businesses that are too directly linked to the economy.

My preference is the health and wellness industry. In an economy that is filled with financial anxiety, people are focusing more on wellness.

According to the U.S. Census Bureau,[1] "Retail sales of personal care and pharmacy stores increased by 15 and 12 percent respectively, while sales of home furnishing and home appliances decreased by 39 and 25 percent as consumers shift focus from home to self."

A recent article on CNBC,[2] suggested that the health and wellness industry is in for even greater growth as a result of the aging baby boomer population:

The health and wellness industries will thrive in the years to come. According to projections by the Centers for Medicare and Medicaid Services, by 2018, national health spending is expected to reach $4.4 trillion and comprise just over one-fifth (20.3 percent) of GDP. This is up from 2009's $2.5 trillion and 17.6 percent.

---

[1] www.moneyanxiety.com/Blog/page1/2011/09/12/57b64d19-1579-4c1ab3d9-61f261757d92.aspx

[2] www.cnbc.com/id/34941331/Bust_of_the_Baby_Boomer_Economy_Generation_Spend_Tightens_Belt

Now, I am no mathematician, but it's pretty easy to see an opportunity when an industry goes from $2.5 trillion to $4.4 trillion in nine years.

There are hundreds of companies in network marketing that categorize themselves as health and wellness companies, but it is easy to narrow the field down to just a few by looking at the research and development (R&D), patents, and peer-reviewed/published papers behind the company's products.

As the economy struggles, it becomes much easier to make sales and create volume if the company has a broad line of impact products.

Some potential growth product areas might include:
o Weight loss
o Green products
o Antiaging
o Sports nutrition
o Daily supplements

- **Corporate Leadership:** This area is one of the most misunderstood in network marketing. Many companies in this industry are owned and/or run by large distributors that left their companies and decided to start their own network. On its face you may think that this dynamic offers you an advantage. I would suggest that the opposite is true. Their call to action is based on the premise "We have been where you are, and we know what you need." Of course there is some truth to that statement; however, I would argue that most distributor-run companies do not possess the skill set required to effectively build a company that can prosper over time.

I am not criticizing the *intentions* of the distributor who wants to launch a company of his or her own. But in my opinion, most big distributors, although good team builders, do not possess the knowledge and experience required to run a global company. To become a billion-dollar company, it is always advantageous to have an ownership/leadership team in place that has already built and run a successful company. When that's the case, there are fewer surprises to deal with. In fact, most executives at that level have already dealt with similar experiences in other settings. In addition, a higher caliber of ownership understands the intricacies of global expansion, R&D, marketing, and distribution. They are also skilled in the area of strategic planning. In my opinion, most distributor-owned companies are much more tactical-oriented than strategically focused.

With these thoughts in mind, let's discuss five traits of company ownership that are important:

1. *Well-financed*: Make sure you are working with people who can sustain the initial period of funding during a launch phase and then are financially secure enough to be able to fund massive growth. Many companies fail for one of two reasons: They are undercapitalized at launch and have slow sales, or they are poorly funded and collapse under the weight of their own success due to a lack of capital. This is one of the main reasons why I suggest finding a company that has been in business for more than 10 years.

2. *Previous experience building and leading a successful company*: Never underestimate the knowledge that comes with previous success. Network marketers are well known for promoting the importance of following people who have "done it before." Make sure you apply those same principles to your ownership's ability to build and lead a global enterprise.

3. *Core competency utilizing various forms of media*: One of the challenges facing network marketing companies today is their lack of experience and knowledge regarding how to use other forms of media to promote their company and its associates. Look for owners who are willing to help tell the story through various forms of advertising and promotion. Many network marketing company owners and executives don't understand the impact of social media, and many of these same companies get their legal advice, policies, and procedures from one group of multilevel marketing, or MLM, attorneys.

   Have you ever wondered why almost every start-up network marketing company has the same policies and procedures? The answer is the same attorneys draw up the policies of most start-ups, and they usually have some rule (that was written many years ago) about using the Internet.

   Most of the time, these rules do not consider the social media world that we live in today, so they are outdated and unfair. Yet, I know a number of people who have been terminated from their company for breaking an outdated rule about posting business information online.

   Ask to see the Internet marketing policies before you sign up for any company.

4. *Access to breakthrough, impact products*: Remember question number one? It is difficult to work in an environment in which the ownership/leadership does not have access to breakthrough products. Due to competition, most companies in this industry have limited access to impact products exclusive to their opportunity. If you can find someone who does, you are miles ahead of the rest of the field.

5. *Reputation:* Look for an ownership team that has a stellar reputation beyond the network marketing *space*. This will offer your associates a higher degree of credibility and a bolstered confidence that they are creating a company that will have more mainstream acceptance.

■ **Field/Team Leadership:** These are the people who are available to help you personally. They are the various levels of associates who have actually done what they are prepared to teach you to do. One of the great challenges in this industry is finding people to team with you who know where to send you for information and support. As a new associate, you need to find a team that offers an extensive hands-on training program that will allow you to learn at your own pace and begin generating product volume quickly—which will allow you to start earning *now*.

Avoid any team that generates large sums of income through the sales of training aids. Google can be a good friend as you search for information. An excellent source of reliable information can be found at www.MLMBlog .net. Keep in mind that you will need to spend some money to build a business of your own, but beware of teams that promote $99 websites and costly CDs and literature. An ideal situation is to team with people who offer a training website that gives you free access to training and motivational information and free downloads. In essence, you do not charge your army for "bullets" . . . you equip them!

Also look for a team that helps you identify your strengths and assists you in building your business through those strengths. Join a team of people who utilize technology for webinars and teleseminars. This offers you the opportunity to reach out to multitudes of people in a single day/night. Make sure you are teamed with people who also blend offline training and team-building events with their use of technology. Find a team that has an in-depth understanding of how to utilize the power of the Internet but also has offline capabilities. Too much reliance on one over the other will not give you the best possible opportunity to succeed. Balance is crucial.

Engage with people who offer you value—people who genuinely serve your best interests. The most dynamic teams are those that are concerned about your success and well-being, and their actions will demonstrate such. Align your future with people who ask you to "give your best and reach your highest." Working with people who share your values is crucial to your long-term success.

Look for a team that is moving forward. Make sure their claims are verifiable. Ask for copies of company newsletters, for example, that reinforce their statements of growth. Look for success that has been duplicated by members of the team, not just the *lone star* that is often highlighted. If they cannot provide this information, look elsewhere.

Just as joining the right company is important, joining the right team in the right company is also key. It might be easier to relate this recommendation to the following example: Playing in the NFL is great; however, if your desire is to become a Super Bowl champion, then is it important to play on the right team.

- **Compensation:** Before we dig into compensation plans, let's see if we agree on the following statement: A 2011 Toyota Camry Hybrid will perform better than a 1959 Edsel.

The fact is that the 2011 will have better performance, will get better gas mileage, and will probably be more attractive to most people. If I am banking on getting from point A to point B and I have a choice to drive the 1959 or the 2011, I am going to choose the 2011 every time.

The car example is not that much different than network marketing compensation plans. For the most part, plans that are thoughtfully constructed or that have recently been revamped will outperform those plans that were constructed years earlier. Having said that, the most effective compensation plans in network marketing today are hybrid plans that take advantage of the best and most attractive attributes of the vast menu of plans that are available.

The fastest-growing companies in the past five years have all had something in common . . . they learn from the past and adapt to today's environment. Some plans have a history of creating great momentum but fail to provide long-term security, whereas others provide long-term security but only for a few of the highest earners. Balance is key when considering what type of plan you want to invest your time in.

Remember, as you listen to a compensation plan explanation from someone, you are likely hearing bits and pieces of what the associate is being taught to say.

Here are some key points to consider when analyzing a compensation plan:

○ **Does the plan offer you the potential to earn your investment back within the first 30 days?** Fast Track cash and other immediate income bonuses are vital to your success in a volatile economy. A person who invests $299 to $599 to get his or her business started should have a clear blueprint about getting that investment back in the first 30 days.

○ **Does the plan offer a balance of motivators?** Cash is a big motivator for many people and you will want access to cash bonuses in the plan, but some people are motivated by other things, such as luxury vacations and car bonuses. Make sure that the plan is well balanced between cash and lifestyle-impacting bonuses.

○ **Is there a clear blueprint that outlines the steps it takes to make the amount of money you are looking for?** In many cases, it is impossible to look at a compensation plan and get a clear picture of the income level you would like to achieve. When questioned about this issue, many longtime networkers will shrug it off and suggest that you "worry about that when you get to that level." I am not the type of person to get bogged down in details, but I do think it's reasonable to have a clear understanding of how the money works before taking a leap of faith and getting started in a business. You wouldn't accept a job without knowing how much money you will be paid, so do not accept a lame answer about how the compensation plan works.

○ **Is the compensation plan well-balanced?** That is, does the plan pay well in the beginning, middle, and back end? The fastest-growing companies today are paying out close to 50 percent of their revenues back to the independent associates, yet there are some companies that publish a payout in the 30 to 35 percent range. One of the largest network marketing companies in the world pays out a little over 30 percent, yet you will find thousands of associates convinced that they have the best compensation plan in the industry. Don't fall for the hype. Find out the true payout and do your own math. As far as I'm concerned, 50 percent is a lot better than 30 percent, but you wouldn't know it if you listened to their pitch.

○ **Does the plan have an incentive for building a customer base?** Companies within the network marketing
industry typically fall into one of two categories: those
that are product-focused or opportunity-focused. The
best-case scenario is finding a company that has a focus
on both categories. Product sales and consumption are
vital to the long-term growth, stability, and residual
income aspects of network marketing. However, I have
been in company meetings that are so product detail–
focused that a doctor had to do the presentation to
explain the science behind the product. Not long ago,
I was invited to take a look at a business and one of the big
sales points was that more than 20 percent of the people
involved are doctors. My friend suggested that the doctors bring a great deal of credibility to the company and
it's products; I don't disagree, but associates in a company like this will tend to expect a doctor to present the
product science at every meeting. And when the doctors
aren't present, the associates tend to stay away. Focusing
solely on the products will produce a loyal group of product users, but it might not produce the income results
that people are looking for. Eventually those loyal product users may look elsewhere. The opposite also occurs.
There are other companies that focus entirely on the
business opportunity and ignore the products. Focusing
on opportunity alone is a recipe for disaster as well. Not
only is it a good way to attract the attention of attorney generals and federal regulators, but it is also a leading factor in the poor retention rate many companies
experience. The best-case scenario is a balance of loyal
customers who enjoy the benefits of the products and

a group of opportunity-driven businesspeople who are looking to spread the word and make more money. Several companies are now offering successful promotions to incentivize customers to refer more customers by offering free product when a referral places an order. The referral promotions are smart for a couple of reasons. First, the company and associates gain more customers. Second, the customers figure out that it is not difficult to refer people to a quality product, and sometimes they will decide to sign up as associates to reap the greater benefits of building a team.

○ **Does the plan consider the very basics of network marketing?** You want to position yourself to create customer volume and bring on new business partners who create volume. Review the percentages you will make on customer volume and the percentages you will make on business partner volume. These percentages, in addition to the overall payout of the plan, will help you determine whether the plan is one that will offer you the best chance for success.

Here is a list of other questions to ask yourself as you consider what company might be best for you:

○ **Does the company culture feel comfortable?** This is certainly objective, but you want to find a home, not a temporary stop on your journey to success.

○ **Is the company publicly traded or privately held?** My personal opinion is that a publically traded company has little choice but to serve the shareholders. The question is whether serving the shareholders of the company also serves the best interest of the associates.

○ **Does the company pay its commissions on time?** One of the guest authors on my blog recently wrote an article about a company whose headquarters were located in a UPS Store (a P.O. box, to be exact). He suggested this was a red flag and warned people about the company. As might be expected, some of the associates wanted to string up our author because he spoke badly about their company. You might be amazed at the reaction you get from people who are financially involved with a company, even when reporting the obvious truth. Not long after the first article was published, we found evidence that this company was actually bouncing commission checks.

○ **Does the company website look professional?** Remember, your image is attached to the image of the company. It's not hard to get a professionally developed website without spending a ton of money today. If the company website looks bad and is filled with spelling errors, it might be a good idea to look elsewhere.

○ **What kind of training and support does the company or upline leadership offer?** As a big believer in training and personal development, I believe it is vital that someone offer training related to getting started, doing a presentation, following up, product knowledge, and so on. Sometimes companies do a good job with this type of training, but most of the time the training and business-building tools are produced by a leader or team in the field. This type of training will make your life a lot easier as you build a large team. You do not want to be spending valuable time going over the same training every day. Your time is better spent by sending your newest associate to a training website while you focus your efforts on individual coaching and business-building activities.

After nearly 20 years of involvement in the industry of network marketing, I would rank the most important attribute of any company or opportunity as security. "Will the company be in business to pay your bonus checks next month?" is probably the most important question that must be answered. Of course, every start-up will attempt to answer the question, but few will have history and facts behind the answer.

Pam and Drew Otto, a couple who made it to the top levels of a start-up company, only to have it close down after two years, are a great example of taking the lessons they learned at the start-up and applying them to a safe and secure company, where they were ranked in the top 10 in growth out of over 1 million distributors.

Pam and Drew rose quickly to one of the top levels in their company by applying skills that they acquired from previous experience. Here is an interview I did with Pam:

Ty Tribble: How were you exposed to the industry of network marketing?

Pam Otto: In the 1990s, I was looking for a new challenge in my life, and I ended up falling in love with the sport of triathlon. As I continued to race, I looked at ways to become faster and stronger and to stay injury free. I was always searching for the best nutrition to put in my body, knowing that what fuel you put in your body will set you apart from the rest on the race course. It was at that time that I was introduced to some network marketing products to help give me an edge as an athlete.

Ty Tribble: So you had success with the products first and then what happened?

Pam Otto: I didn't really know anything about the industry, but I felt like the products were really great. So I ended up researching the opportunity that came along with the products and I was really intrigued. My immediate goal was to make enough money to pay for my products, and after accomplishing that goal in less than 24 hours, I was really starting to think about what I stumbled upon. Not only did I achieve my goal of paying for my products, but I also made a small profit on the first day.

Ty Tribble: What made you turn the corner and look at network marketing as a serious business opportunity?

Pam Otto: I quickly learned that if I applied just a little effort, I could actually make a real income in this industry. And at that point, I said, "Game on!" My goal was to be a full-time mom. At the time I was working three long days in thriving orthodontic practice where we saw more than 100 patients a day, and I would come home exhausted from my days. I was also missing out on events/volunteering in my daughters's life because I was working. So I got to work, putting my plan into motion.

Ty Tribble: You mention your plan. Talk about what you mean by "your plan."

Pam Otto: As an athlete I immediately went to the strategic approach on how to be successful quickly and took what I was doing in my triathlon training, transferred it to this industry, and found a very quick solid success because of a few similarities. One of the similarities is having a coach. One of the turning points for me as a triathlete came in the form of a Mother's Day present when my husband hired a triathlon coach for me. Shortly after my coach was hired, my racing career dramatically changed. I went from competing in my age group to an elite triathlete in just one year. Having the direction of a coach, focus, and the amount of training I put in was my key to success, and the same thing applies to the network marketing industry.

Ty Tribble: I find a lot of people, especially professionals, tend to want to "learn for themselves" and "go it alone" in network marketing. Tell me more about finding the right coach to help you with your business.

Pam Otto: I knew I needed to find a mentor/coach. . . . I needed someone to hold me accountable to my goals and plan on a weekly basis. This is what set me apart in triathlon, and I found the same rang true in my business. The coaching I received on how to build a business set me apart from many who weren't using a mentor.

Ty Tribble: Once you had a coach in place, what else helped you grow your business so quickly?

Pam Otto: I dove headfirst into the training. The training available to build a business is accessible to everyone, but you have to make a choice to put the time into the training to make yourself successful. Not only did I seek out new training, but I would continue to review trainings I had already gone through. I would always take something new away from trainings I had previously done and heard it differently because I had grown from a personal development perspective as the time passed.

Ty Tribble: You have accomplished your goal of quitting your job and becoming a full-time mom along with some other great rewards over the past 24 months, yet you are still a busy mom with lots of activities going on in your life. Talk about how you schedule your time.

Pam Otto: My calendar is one of the most important assets in my business. I am able to see how many home meetings, three-way calls, and one-on-ones I do on a weekly and monthly basis. If I am not finding success, I am able to show my mentor what I did that month and we can determine what I may need to do differently to achieve my goals.

Ty Tribble: You just mentioned your goals again, and I noticed you mentioned goals early on, for example, the goal of paying for your products. Talk about goal setting.

Pam Otto: No getting around it; setting your goals is instrumental to success. You also need to share those goals with your mentor so he or she knows what you are striving to achieve and can then decide how best to help you reach your potential.

Ty Tribble: Thanks so much for sharing with us today, Pam. Anything else you would like to add?

Pam Otto: I was able to find immediate success in the industry because I applied what worked for me as I had success in the past. I was able to quit my job to be home for my husband and daughters. My business paid for two new cars for our family, and I am able to give more to important charities than I would have ever imagined. This industry allows so many people to be able to dream again and shoot for the stars! I know that every person reading this has the ability to achieve great things, and I can't wait to applaud their success.

Now that you have a clear picture of where the network marketing industry is going in the future and you have some criteria that will help you find a quality mentor and company, let's move on to a specific game plan that will help you achieve the results are you looking for.

PART

II

Your Action Plan

BEFORE WE UNPACK the action plan, it's important to remember what to focus on. The previous chapter talked about gaining a clear understanding of why you want to double your income and build financial security outside of your current career. The action plan is quite simple, but as in any worthy endeavor, you will run into roadblocks.

The biggest battle you will fight is within yourself. You battle your thoughts and in some cases years of thinking that you are not talented enough, good-looking enough, or smart enough to achieve great results in your life. Our beliefs guide our decisions and behavior, and many times these limiting beliefs begin to form at a very young age.

Henry Ford said, "If you think you can do a thing or think you can't do a thing, you're right."

Think about the words you choose very carefully, especially when you talk to yourself. Many people tear themselves apart in their heads every day and fail to realize that they are acting as their own worst enemy. Rather than saying, "I'm not sure that is possible," try saying, "With a little time and effort, I can accomplish anything."

Everyone has hard times, everyone has things that don't go his or her way, and everyone experiences setbacks. But for every person on earth who experiences these things, you can find another who has battled back from similar circumstances. A worthwhile dream or goal will always come with a price. You are not alone in your desire to improve your life and your family's financial future.

The following action steps are the basics of building your long-term business. These basics have been proven over the past 30-plus years. Technologies and trends change, but the basics remain the same—and they always work. In later chapters we discuss today's technology and trends, but first it is vital that you have a good foundation in the basics.

4

Building a Never-Ending List of Prospects

Your list of potential business partners and customers is the lifeblood of your business. The first step in making a list of names is really a brainstorming process. Your goal is to get as many names that you can remember written down on paper or entered into a spreadsheet or database. Whatever you do, do not prejudge anyone. Although some of the people you include may not be interested in starting a business, many of them will know someone else who is interested.

Your list of names will be used as much for referrals as for finding actual business partners and customers. In some cases you might remember only a person's first name; in other cases, you might not remember a name at all. In these cases, create a placeholder, for example, "the guy who mows my neighbor's lawn on Thursday afternoon."

Many people have lists already compiled for various reasons. These might include:

- Facebook
- Wedding invitation list
- High school, college annual
- Church directory

In the world of Internet marketing, a list is typically housed with an autoresponder service. We discuss this in Chapter 14. But it is important to remember that some people on your team will want to build their business using the latest technology, and others on your team want nothing to do with technology. Many people are very successful using only a phone, a pen, and yellow notepad.

Your goal should be to write down 100 to 300 people's names, but the actual number is not as important as it once was. When I first got started in the industry in the 1990s, the list was the only thing you had. Once my list of names dwindled, I hit what I call the warm market wall, and things began to feel very difficult.

I began to procrastinate because I knew that my list of names was very small. I felt as if I made one more call, my list was going to be empty. At the time, there were only a handful of methods to add people to your list. My mentor's favorite method was to "go meet people." I think back on those times when I would go to the mall and wander around for hours, hoping to bump into someone that I could "prospect." Think about it; the very best, most up-to-date method of finding people to do business with was to stalk people at the mall. And almost everyone in network marketing was being taught the same methods, so it became a free-for-all on the poor jewelry counter lady.

Today, we live in a different world, which is one of the reasons why I believe that the Social Marketing Revolution is taking place. It's a lot easier to locate and reach out to a few people a day on Facebook than it was to stalk the mall or drive to 10 different gas stations in one night, hoping to strike up a conversation with someone pumping gas. We devote more time to Facebook in Chapter 16.

Another great way to add names to your list is by using a memory jogger.

Write down who you know in the following occupations:

Accounting (CPA) _____

Acupuncture _____

Advertising _____

Animal care/grooming _____

Artist _____

Assisted living (home care) _____

Attorney _____

Automotive sales/service _____

Banking _____

Barista (coffee) _____

Carpet sales/cleaning _____

Caterer _____

Chiropractor _____

Clothing sales/design/manufacturing _____

Coaching _____

Computer sales/service _____

Construction _____

Counselor _____

Courier _____

Dentist _____

Doctor _____

Dry cleaner _____

Electrician _____

Engineer _____

Financial planning _____

Florist _____

Funeral home _____

Furniture sales _____

Garden shop _____

Glass sales/replacement _____

Golf instructors _____

Hair salon _____

Health spa _____

Heating/air conditioning _____

Insurance _____

Janitor _____

Landscaping _____

Massage therapist_____

Mortgage _____

Moving and storage _____

Office supply_____

Painting _____

Pest control _____

Pharmacy _____

Photography _____

Picture framing _____

Plumber _____

Real estate _____

Roofing _____

Security systems _____

Signs _____

Telephone/wireless phone _____

Titles and escrow_____

Travel agent _____

Tree service _____

Veterinarian _____

Video and sound _____

Wedding coordinator _____

Network marketing as a term has been used for decades, but few people really think about the term and actually apply the first word (or the second word for that matter).

Bob Burg, author of the *Go-Giver* and *Endless Referrals*, describes *networking* as "the cultivating of mutually beneficial, give and take, win/win relationships." Whether you predominantly utilize social media or face-to-face meetings, the art of building relationships is one of the most important aspects of building a profitable business.

10 Tips That Will Help You Become a Better Networker

1. *Give value without any thought of what you might get back in return.* One of the greatest things about giving has to do with reciprocity. The social psychology term refers to the fact that a positive action will many times be met with a positive action. If you give someone a referral for his or her business, that person will want to do the same for you.
2. *Always speak respectfully about your competition.* Do not be afraid to differentiate yourself from your competition, but keeping conversations on the positive shows confidence, maturity, and success.
3. *Focus on helping people get what they want.* This one is easy to say and much more difficult to implement. To implement this in your daily life, simply ask more questions, talk less, and listen more.
4. *Encourage others at every opportunity.* Sometimes you will see talent in people who fail to recognize it themselves. Your encouragement can make a big difference.
5. *Be kind.* Plato said, "Always be kind, for everyone is fighting a hard battle." We really never know what is going on

in a person's life, and your kind words might make all the difference in the world for someone.

6. *Take the time to genuinely get to know people*. Showing a genuine interest in the well-being of others will set you apart from the crowd and make people remember you.

7. *Invite people to lunch and host dinner parties*. Lunch and dinner are great ways to put your networking into practice. Dinner parties are a wonderful way to connect other people. The better you are at connecting others, the more business will flow your way.

8. *Be generous with your time and resources*. Volunteering your time for a cause that you believe in is a surefire way to meet people who share the same values and interests that you do. Volunteer because you want to give back and then enjoy the rewards of networking with other like-minded people.

9. *Do not be afraid to go deep and meaningful*. Getting into meaningful conversations is a great way to be remembered and a wonderful way to show that you truly care for others.

10. *Remember names*. A couple of simple tricks that will help you remember people's names are to repeat the name both in your head and then in a sentence back to the person. For example, instead of just saying, "It's nice to meet you," you can say, "It's nice to meet you, John." Repeating John's name in your head will also help you remember. Another technique that many people use is to associate the person with what they do for fun or for a living. If you learn that John is a volunteer baseball coach, repeating, "John, baseball coach" in your head will help you associate John's name with him.

You can network anywhere, including online and on social media. The choice is yours, but the simple principles of true networking still work regardless of the media you choose.

5

The Art and Science of Contacting and Inviting

WORDS ARE IMPORTANT, and although I am a big believer in scripts, word tracks, and agendas, it is also vital that you start with the right mind-set.

The proper mind-set will have a tremendous impact on your ability to communicate effectively with your potential business partners. Many people within the industry of network marketing will refer to your mind-set as your posture. We are not talking about physical posture, but rather an attitude or frame of mind.

The right attitude and mind-set begin with your belief, and we can break down belief into three areas.

1. *Gain belief in the industry of network marketing.* Hopefully this book will give you confidence in the industry as a whole. There is simply no denying the success of an industry that does in excess of $114 billion in sales worldwide. According to the Direct Selling Association, a whopping, 74 percent of Americans have purchased products from this channel of distribution.

2. *Gain belief in your company of choice.* The chapter on choosing the right company outlines what to look for. Once you've made a quality decision based on all available information, put your blinders on and run with that company. Changing companies on a regular basis, based on a "grass is always greener" attitude, is a good way to delay your success for a long time. I have been put in the situation where I had no choice but to change companies, and it was not a fun experience. You will lose volume, customers, and associates with every move. I listed security as one of the top things to look for in a company because I have experienced insecurity and chaos in the past. Once you find the

right company, get to know the high-income earners in the company so that your belief level in the income potential rises.

3. *Have a strong belief in yourself and your own capabilities.* If you lack belief in yourself, my suggestion is to attend a conference or find the profiles of successful people within your company. Once you read the success stories and see the pictures of other successful associates with your company, you will likely have an "If they can do it, I can do it" moment.

   It might also help you if you devoted a few pages of your goals and dreams notebook to some notes on why you chose your company along with some notes about meeting high-income earners and company representatives. Your dreams and goals notebook will become a wonderful scrapbook that many people on your future team will enjoy reading as you achieve different levels of success.

Once you have belief in the industry, your company, and yourself, the next step is to begin to translate that belief into excitement and enthusiasm for your business.

There is a very fine line between genuine excitement for your business and the type of excitement that scares people. Most of you will remember the cartoon bird spokesperson for Cocoa Puffs cereal. Sonny, the cuckoo bird, would try all kinds of things to contain his excitement level about Cocoa Puffs cereal and then he would inevitably go coo-coo and elevate to a scary level of enthusiasm for sugary breakfast food. We are not talking about coo-coo for Cocoa Puffs level excitement. We are talking about a genuine and authentic excitement in your voice and a detectible level of confidence when you speak.

Seven Attributes of Effective Business Posture

1. *Your business does not rise and fall based on the actions of any given person except yourself.* The best posture to take is that you really don't care whether a person gets involved with you in your business or not. You are looking for people who want to make a major impact on their lives and the lives of thousands of people. If the prospect does not see your vision, you will find someone who does. The outcome of the meeting is much less important than actions you take to fill up your calendar. You cannot fail if you do enough of the right things.

2. *You look at your contacting and presenting as an interview instead of a presentation.* You are interviewing the other person to see if he or she qualifies to be part of your business. Never beg a person to come to a meeting or ask someone to do you a favor by listening to your presentation. Begging and asking for a favor is a demonstration of lower personal value. Your time and your business have high value, so you must act that way from the beginning. You have everything at your disposal to create a multimillion-dollar business, so the best way to look at your business is that you already have a multimillion-dollar business in its infancy.

3. *You smile and laugh!* In his book, *How to Win Friends and Influence People*, Dale Carnegie says: "The effect of a smile is powerful—even when it is unseen. Telephone companies throughout the United States have a program called 'phone power' which is offered to employees who use the telephone for selling their services or products. In this program they suggest that you smile when talking on the phone. Your 'smile' comes through in your voice." Network marketing is actually a lot like dating. You want to give

a great impression, and smiling is the very best way to accomplish this. Remember, our voices project a different tone when we are smiling, so it is equally (or perhaps more so) important to smile while talking on the phone. Have you ever tried to smile and think of a negative thought at the same time? It's virtually impossible to genuinely smile while thinking of something negative. Your smile can relay an optimism in the future that many people might be lacking in today's economic conditions.

Just about every legitimate high-level income earner that I have met in the industry of network marketing has a sense of humor that goes along with the ability to laugh at themselves. People who are generally frustrated and upset with the world are, for the most part, no fun to be around. You are looking to attract people to you, not repel people from you. In simple terms, make a decision to be happy and stick with it.

4. *You are comfortable with you.* Many people are constantly worried about what other people think about them, and the reality is that most people are not thinking all that much about you. People tend to be more concerned with what you are thinking about them. Be relaxed and comfortable in your own skin. We all can be vulnerable in some ways. Rather than focus inwardly on your own deficiencies, work to focus on the other person. A key to success in network marketing is to take your eyes off of yourself and focus on the other people around you. This not only applies to prospecting but also applies a great deal to team building. When you focus on the success of those on your team, you will naturally achieve the success you are looking for.

5. *You pay attention to your physical appearance.* Have good fashion sense and do not dress in sloppy clothes. Some

companies are more formal than others, so it is important to pay attention to the overall culture of a company. As a leader I would suggest that you dress a step above the culture. In other words, if the company culture is jeans and T-shirts, I would suggest you wear slacks and polo shirt. If the culture is business casual with sports coats, slacks, and a button-up shirt, you might want to dress in a suit with a tie.I do not recommend showing up to your buddy's house in a suit and tie if he is used to seeing you in shorts and a T-shirt, though, even if the company culture is professional dress.

If you feel completely lost when it comes to fashion, try going to a department store like Nordstrom or Macy's and ask for help. Tell the salesperson your exact situation and let him or her know that you want to dress to impress.

If you are involved with a more formal company, you will likely have meetings that are business dress and perhaps business casual dress. In this case you can maximize your clothing budget by picking up a high-quality navy suit, a pair of khaki slacks, and a pair of light gray slacks. This combination will give you three different outfits that you can wear with the navy suit jacket. You can wear the suit, the navy jacket and khaki slacks, or the navy jacket with the gray slacks. Pick up a couple of ties and a couple of white shirts along with black shoes, and you are ready for any and all meetings. Last, match your socks to your pants and you will be in good shape.

Your success has a lot to do with impressions, so be sure to pay attention to the little details of grooming, something men sometimes ignore. Wear clean clothing and have a look in the mirror once in a while. Ear hair and nose hair can get out of hand quickly, so pay attention to that stuff, too. Also, men, you don't want Sasquatch-like chest hair sticking out of your shirt collars.

For women, I suggest dressing a step above the culture and watch the necklines. You don't want to be a distraction to a business meeting. That's all I am going to say about women and dress, they are usually not a problem.

6. *You speak to others with volume and confidence.* People perceive soft voices as lacking power and confidence. If you find people straining to hear you, speak up and project your voice. Also make sure to use proper English and enunciate your words clearly. Experienced public speakers can vary the volume of their speech in order to have a greater impact on the audience. However, inexperienced speakers often speak entirely too softly for the audience. The best way to learn how to speak is to study other speakers as often as possible.

7. *You exude a high level of urgency.* Urgency is a powerful tool that you can use to build your business fast. You want your business to be looked at like a fast-moving train. Every once in a while you will slow down to let someone on board, but you are not going to be waiting around for someone who is sitting on the fence, unable to decide whether to jump on board with you. Your personal sense of urgency can be relayed to others by walking and talking a little faster, minimizing procrastination, and focusing on the important tasks that make a difference on your dreams and goals.

Once you have the proper mind-set and posture, the inviting process becomes easy. You will achieve success as long as you are willing to put in the work and go through the numbers.

Contacting Friends and Family

When inviting a friend or family member to look at your business, it is important to remember whom you are talking to. You must be your authentic self, or you run the risk of alienating your closest friends and family members. Remember, if the business or product is good enough for you to get excited about, it is good enough for your friends and family to get excited about.

Avoid saying things like "opportunity" or "expanding your business."

My friend, Todd Falcone, talks about a pattern that many network marketers participate in. He calls this the NFL.

The NFL for this example does not refer to the National Football League, but rather the "no friends left" camp of network marketing. These are network marketers whose friends fret about picking up the phone because they know the call is going to be all business.

Todd has been involved in the network marketing industry for more than 20 years and has some suggestions for steering clear of the NFL:

- Find a (great) company and stick with it.
- Make the commitment to do it. (Do or die.)
- Use the proper, professional approach.
- Pay attention to clues.
- Don't ever chase.

The first three points are self-explanatory, but let's dig a little further into Todd's last two points.

First, pay attention to clues. This is a great point because many people tend to put their blinders on and focus solely on what they are trying to accomplish while paying little attention to the thoughts and feelings of anyone else. People who are not interested in your business will give off clues. It is not your goal to convince or manipulate anyone into joining your business. That is a quick and easy way to turn people off. It is your goal to find people who are already looking for an opportunity to achieve their dreams and goals while making a positive impact on others.

Second, let's tackle the don't-ever-chase suggestion. Here Todd is referring to the act of chasing after your prospects with multiple follow-up phone calls even when it appears obvious that the prospect is not interested in returning your call. I never leave more than two voicemails for someone and never on the same day.

Once a friend or family member expresses lack of interest, I don't bring up the topic again unless I am asked or it naturally comes up in conversation. Your friends and family will really begin to notice something is different once you begin to see rewards from your business. Many will choose to join you at that time, and some will never choose to join you.

Don't worry. There are plenty of people in the world today who are looking for an opportunity and you don't need everyone to join you.

Here are some examples of how to approach someone with an invitation.

Basic Business Approach

"Hey, Bob, this is Ty. I am working with the (Founding Member, for example) of a business organization called (The Pinnacle Group [my team name]). I was with him (or her) the other day and he (or she) told me to identify a few key people who I think want to make some significant money this year and I thought of you. I have no idea if you would even be interested, but if you are open to the idea, why don't we sit down over a cup of coffee and I'll run some numbers by you? If you like what you see, I'll give you some information and we can talk later. If not, no big deal."

The last sentence, "If not, no big deal," is very powerful. You are showing that you are not emotionally attached to the outcome of the conversation. This puts the potential business partner at ease and may even help develop curiosity.

Product-Related Approach

"Mary, this is Ty. Do you remember the other day when you said your knees were hurting you? (Or lack of focus, being sluggish, need to lose weight, etc.) I was thinking about what you said, and I got my hands on a product that I think will help. I have a couple samples and some information for you. When is a good time for me to drop this off? If it works for you I can tell you where to get them at wholesale."

Third-Party Call (calling someone for one of your team)

"Fred, this is Bo Short. You don't know me, but we have a mutual friend, Joe Jones. Joe and I are working with the Chairman (Executive Board Member . . . one of the leaders) of a new business organization called (The Pinnacle Group). We were talking with him (or her) the other day and he (or she) told us to identify a couple key people who we think want to make some significant money this year and Joe thought of you. I don't know you, but if you are open to the idea, why don't the three of us get together and I'll run some numbers by you? If you have interest, we'll talk further. If not, no big deal."

Invitation to a Meeting

> "Mary, this is Bo Short. What are you doing Monday night at eight PM? I am working with the Chairman (one of the leaders) of a business organization called (The Pinnacle Group). I was talking with him (or her) the other day and he (or she) told me to identify a couple key people who I think want to make some significant money this year and I thought of you. He (or she) is going to be in town Monday night (or going to be conducting a live streaming broadcast on the Internet) explaining what we are doing. I want you to meet him (or her) in case you have some interest. If you are intrigued, we can talk about all of the details later. If not, no big deal."

Getting Referrals

Asking for referrals is one of the most powerful yet underused strategies in building a network marketing business. Those who make asking for referrals a part of their everyday business building often see amazing results, but I am truly baffled at the low number of people who use this strategy.

Asking for a referral is very simple. Let's say, for example, that your company offers a joint health product and you have a friend who swears by the product. Asking that friend for a referral is a great way to increase your business.

You might say, "Bill, who do you know who has knee problems similar to yours?" The key words in that sentence are "who do you know." Those four words can be worth a huge amount of profit for your business. Referrals can work for the business opportunity as well. Let's say that you showed your presentation to Janice, but the timing wasn't right for her. By asking

Janice a "who do you know" question, you might open the door in more areas than you can imagine.

Here's an example of what you might say to Janice: "Janice, I know that you are extremely busy as the chair for the school auction, so the timing may not be right for you, but who do you know who is a mom who might be looking to earn some extra money in the next couple of months?"

Notice how I was very specific when I asked the "who do you know" question. I believe the more specific you are, the better. Being specific will get the brain churning, making it more likely that the person you are speaking to will come up with a specific name for you.

One of the hidden benefits of referrals is that when Janice's friend Leah decides to get join your team, you have the ability to go back to Janice and tell her that Leah has decided to get started. You can then ask Janice if she would like to make the overrides on the business that Leah brings to the table. Many companies have an immediate fast start type of bonus that would make it a no-brainer for Janice to get started.

The only way to reap the benefits of referrals is to make it a habit at the end of every meeting to ask, "Who do you know?"—and remember to be specific with your question.

Cold Contacting

Cold contacting used to be all we had. I remember leaving my house wearing a suit and tie on a mission to go meet people. My list of potential business partners had dwindled down to crossed-out names on a yellow notepad, and I was desperate to find new people who might be interested in building a business of their own.

The problem was, I didn't know the words to say to people. The only real training I got at the time, other than to go meet people and compliment them, was to pretend the target looked familiar as a way to strike up a conversation. It felt dishonest and slimy.

After five years of working my tail off and struggling with cold contacting, I took a bit of a sabbatical from the industry. But when I returned, I not only brought my skills related to Internet marketing but found a new mentor named Bo Short who had a real system for contacting people. Bo's "It's Called Practice" training has been translated into 10 languages and heard by millions of people around the world.

The basics of the strategy are to make cold contacting as simple and easy as asking someone for directions. Bo developed this script after being frustrated by driving seven hours one way, only to have his potential business partner not show.

Bo's Script

Bo: Excuse me, can you help me? My name is Bo Short. Are you from (name the town)?

Joe: Yes.

Bo: Fantastic, maybe you can help me out. I am in the process of expanding a business in the area and I'm looking for a go-getter type, someone who would not be opposed to making an extra 2 to 3 thousand dollars a month. Do you know anyone like that?"

(While asking the last question, reach into your pocket and take out a business card.)

You will now hear one of several answers.

Possible Answers

- No.
- I might be interested; depends on what it is.
- Yes, I know someone.
- No thanks, I am not interested.

How You Answer Each One

- Great, thanks for your time.
- I am in a hurry right now, but write your name and number on the back of my card and I will call you when I get a chance.
- I am in a hurry right now, but write their name and number on the back of my card and I will call them when I get a chance. By the way, who can I say referred them?
- That's okay, I wasn't talking about you; do you know anyone like that?

The beauty of Bo's approach is that there's absolutely no rejection involved. If the other person doesn't know anyone, you treat it as if you asked him or her for directions to the nearest Starbucks and the person doesn't know because he or she isn't a coffee drinker. No one on earth would feel rejected or down when asking for directions; they would simply ask someone else. This strategy changed everything for me and propelled me on to new heights in a very short time.

How to Handle Invite Objections and Questions

Handling the questions that come up during the inviting process is usually something that strikes fear into the hearts of every networker. But if you have the answers, then it is really only a matter of practice before you feel comfortable.

There are really three questions that come up over and over again during the inviting process. These answers apply to my particular business, but it will be fairly easy to insert the information from your company if we are not involved with the same business or team. Get together with some of your leaders and put together your own script based on what follows.

Question #1: "What is it?"

Response: "It's called the Pinnacle Group. It consists of community leaders from around the country working with a brand partner expanding their 300 products into seven countries. Have you ever heard of it?"

Question #2: "No, what's that all about?"

Response: "Oh, that's the easy part. When we get together I'll run through all the information and leave you some products and literature. If you have some interest we'll talk further; if not, no big deal."

Question #3: "What is it exactly?"

Response: "Have you ever heard of a guy named Roger Barnett? His family owns Burberry, one of the top five luxury fashion brands in the United States. He also owned Beauty.com. In fact, if you ever opened a magazine with the perfume samples inside, that was his company as well. In 2004 he bought our brand partner. Have you ever heard of the Shaklee Corporation? He purchased them in 2004. Did you hear what they did in October 2010?"

Remember, your goal is not to answer every question a person has. Your goal is to schedule a meeting.

6

Double Your Income Bonus Chapter

Insider Secrets to Recruiting
Professionals with Todd Falcone

THE KEY TO SUCCESS in network marketing is building a big team of self-reliant, responsible producers who have both the willingness and the capacity to do what we do on a daily basis and then take those abilities and turn them into productivity.

One of the biggest challenges facing network marketers is in finding good people. In fact, many people end up asking themselves, "Where in the world are all the good people? I keep working and can't seem to find people who duplicate."

The solution to that is in specifically targeting good people. Network marketing is a social business that is driven by people talking to people. So . . . it makes sense then to specifically focus on "people" people.

Our natural human tendency is to take the path of least resistance. If the road is easier, we take it. Unfortunately, what most people *think* is the path of least resistance is actually the path of greatest resistance. New network marketers often think it is easier to talk to their broke friends and family because they need an opportunity and because they perceive that process to be much less frightening than going after talented individuals.

The primary problem with that thought process is that when you go after broke people, you tend to be met with far more resistance than you do by going after successful people. Your broke friends tend to me more hesitant and skeptical based on their personal life choices. Successful people are successful for good reason. They are open to opportunities . . . and they seize them.

Many years ago, through my own experience working leads and becoming increasingly frustrated with having to sort through individuals who didn't even remotely have the capability to do what we do in this profession, I began to ask myself, "What can I do where I put myself in the position of talking to *only* professional people?"

The answer was sitting on my desk in the form of a real estate publication. I thought to myself, "Hmm . . . realtors. They're all hardworking, outgoing, and make money on commissions and prospect like we do. I wonder how they'll respond if I call them."

That was the beginning of a journey that I am still on today—a method that is now my primary way of finding talent for my business. It's one that I am asked to teach whenever I speak and use to train network marketing professionals around the world.

Think about it. Your objective is to find good people. Good people are working. Not only are you looking for good people, but you're looking for people who essentially do what we do in network marketing. This method is about prospect profiling, about going after people who are more likely to be successful in network marketing based on what they do already. People who sell for a living, earn based on their own personal productivity, and have a moderate to high tolerance for risk are ideal for what we do in this profession.

Recruiting talented producers is actually far easier than recruiting those who have shown little or no upward mobility in their careers. Once you begin recruiting *up* the socioeconomic chain, you'll never go down again. And, you'll quickly realize that any fears you had related to calling those individuals dissipate after one or two phone calls because of what you're met with: receptivity. Successful people are open to opportunity. It is how they became successful in the first place. And, once you become successful, you typically become even more open to opportunities that come across your desk.

Certain career categories are ideally suited for what we do as network marketers, including realtors, professional salespeople, insurance agents, mortgage brokers, small-business owners, as well as others in a variety of managerial positions.

These people do what we do. They sell, lead, oversee, and inspire every day. And, they get paid the way we get paid. If they produce or their team produces, they make more money. If they don't, they earn less. They talk to people, are social creatures, have major responsibilities in their occupation, and are driven and motivated by money. They've chosen those careers because of what they offer: upward mobility.

And remember this: Just because someone is in a job or career doesn't mean that he or she isn't open to looking at your business. Timing is everything for everyone. If you pick up the phone and ask, you'll start getting answers. The more you prospect—the more you ask—the bigger your check will grow.

Prospecting should be fun. Most people unfortunately don't see it that way because of the massive amount of sorting we have to go through to find good people. With this particular method, pretty much everyone you talk to sounds good and has the goods to make things happen. Imagine if every time you picked up the phone to make a prospecting call, the person on the other end of the line sounded like someone you'd be thrilled to have in your business seven days a week. How much fun would you have now? Compare that to some of the calls you've made in the past when you happen to get on the phone with someone who can't even carry on a conversation and the first words out of his or her mouth are, "How much is this gonna cost me?" Prospecting *up* the socioeconomic chain to professional people who already sell or manage for a living is not only fun but a much faster way for you to find productive people to add to your team.

There are literally millions and millions of people who are moving in and through these career categories that I mentioned. And they are very easy to find in your local market, as well as regionally, nationally, and even internationally. If you wanted to find a realtor in Chicago, for example, it would be pretty easy for you to simply hop onto Google and type in "Chicago real estate agents," wouldn't it? What if you wanted to find insurance agents, mortgage brokers, or people who sell cars? Do you think you could find one? Easy.

Then, once you locate them, you simply pick up the phone, pique the prospect's interest, and ask a question.

I spent nearly six years perfecting the following question to pique interest, and I still use it today:

"Do you at all keep your options open in terms of making any money outside of what you are currently doing in the _____ profession?"

If I drive by a real estate sign, I slow down and write the realtor's name and phone number on a yellow notepad I keep in my car. I put on the gas, make the call, and ask that question. Students of mine who do this exactly as I teach it have an average positive response rate of about 50 percent—that is, about half of the people they call say "yes" to that question. Can you imagine? Everyone you call sounds good. In fact, they all sound like someone you'd love to have in your business, and *half* of them say "yes" to you? Compare that with some of the other methods you might be using in your business today.

Recruiting up is powerful. When you decide to begin targeting talent rather than sharing your story with anyone who is willing to listen, you'll start having more fun and undoubtedly begin sponsoring more quality. When you recruit up, you create a culture of doers. It dramatically reduces prospecting frustration and aggravation. It shortens the learning curve for new reps because they already know how to sell and manage. And, it accelerates organizational growth potential. The more producers you put into your business, the more production you're going to have in your business.

There's one final and highly significant concept I'd like to add to this method that is sure to put you over the top. I know that some people reading this may be thinking, "But . . . I'm not making any money yet. Why would *these* people even listen to me? I'm new to this whole thing. How would anyone of this caliber ever want to join *me?*" Remember this and take ownership in it. These people don't know you; they don't know your background, where you live, or how much money you make. I earned my first five-figure monthly check working out of my garage. My prospects didn't know it. Why? I didn't tell them, nor did I act like it.

Perception is projection. Remember that. Your prospects' reality of you is what you project upon them. How you act, what you say and do, is all a matter of choice. If you choose to act successful, responsible, and on your game, you'll be perceived as such. So, when it comes to recruiting these types of individuals, you get to decide what their reality or experience with you is all about. Just because you're broke or not yet successful doesn't mean you have to act like it. If you act successful, you'll be perceived as such. This doesn't mean that you lie to people and tell them you're making a bunch of money when you're not; it means acting the part until you become it. How would you act if you were making five figures a month? Would it be different than the way you act today? If so, act as if you're already there, and you'll find yourself more easily attracting quality, successful people into your business.

Do yourself a favor and start recruiting up. Become a talent scout. Start looking for good people. Throw away the concept of talking to anyone and everyone who is simply willing to hear you out. If you were the chief executive officer (CEO) of a company and you had to hire a president to run it, someone who was responsible, had a proven track record, and was willing to do whatever it took, no matter how long it took to get the job done, would you hire just anyone who walked in the door? Of course not. You'd hire the *best* person for the job. Start looking for better people. This is your business. You get to choose whom you talk to and whom you bring in.

When you begin applying this method in your daily marketing efforts, you'll no doubt smile more, laugh more, and sponsor more. Not only that, you'll be bringing in people who can get the job done. We all want good people in our downline . . . and now you have a specific method to apply to help you get them.

This information comes from The Insider Secrets to Recruiting Professionals, Todd's #1 selling training program. For more details, simply visit: www.ToddFalcone.com.

Ty Tribble: You have been in the network marketing industry for more than 20 years. Talk about what is different today versus when you first got started.

Todd Falcone: What's different today more than anything are the tools and technologies available to us. When I first got started, the Internet didn't even exist. We built by doing group meetings, one-on-ones, conference calls, and fax-on-demand. Along comes the Internet, and with it, a lot more choices. I do think it is both a blessing and a curse . . . more blessing than curse, though. With it comes choices, confusion, and distraction. So . . . in today's market, we've got to work harder at keeping our troops focused on the task at hand, building a downline, and selling our stuff. For sure, we also have our business-building lives greatly enhanced with online videos, autoresponders, blogs, squeeze pages, and other online mechanisms to help us drive. So . . . the short answer, what's different? We now have the 'Net . . . and I like it.

Ty Tribble: What does a typical day look like for you?

Todd Falcone: Gym, breakfast with the kids, then get them to the bus stop and school. After that, I walk into my office, check e-mail, glance at Facebook, then start making calls. I'm on the phone most of the day and in front of my computer all the time. I do a lot of writing and video production for my training company, and I try to reserve that stuff for later at night when people are sleeping and not reachable. I spend my daylight hours when people are alert and moving around talking to them and my nighttime hours doing creative stuff . . . things that are more indirectly related to revenue production.

Ty Tribble: What is the most spontaneous thing you have ever done given your time and financial freedom?

Todd Falcone: I was in Hawaii for a few days speaking for a client and staying at a friend's house who is a rep for that company. After we got out of the water from surfing that morning, my friend Gordo looked at me from across the room and said, "Hey, you wanna jump out of a plane today?" My response was immediate. I said "Absolutely!" He yelled back to his wife and said, "Honey, you wanna jump out of a plane with me and Todd today?" She said yes and two hours later we were hopping out of a plane from 14,000 feet. Super fun.

Ty Tribble: I've seen you in action, on the phone, and you are an animal. But I know it wasn't always like that. How did you get over your initial fear of picking up the phone and talking to people?

Todd Falcone: Everybody has phone fear when they start out. It's unknown and different when you're now out there talking to people about a business or a cool product they can buy. You make a call and stink at it. You make another and stink . . . just a little less. There's nothing like call after call after call to help the fear go away. One step at a time . . . one call or meeting at a time. The thing is, you have to *want* success bad enough to make the call. I wanted it, so in spite of how I felt and how intimidated I was, I did it anyway.

Ty Tribble: What is your system for following up with potential customers and business partners?

Todd Falcone: My system? High-tech, man. I talk to them . . . show them some initial information. Then, if they need more, I get it to them and book a firm time to get back to them . . . soon. I don't wait a week. I call them as soon as possible. How soon is possible? It depends for every prospect. So, the key thing for me is to follow up in a very timely manner. Prospects lose respect for you if you don't follow up with them. They expect it. So I guess I just do my best to live up to their expectations of them wanting me to call them back and sign them up in my business!

Ty Tribble: You have taken a lot of trips because of your business. What trip was your favorite?

Todd Falcone: Ty, I have traveled so many places and so many times that it is hard to pick a favorite. I have had a blast all over the world hanging out with people in our profession. But, if you're making me pick one, it would be Thailand and Singapore. My Asia trip this year was off-the-charts fun. Great people, super food—everything about it was fun. I'm ready to go back again soon.

Ty Tribble: How do you see the network marketing industry evolving in the next 20 years?

Todd Falcone: How do I see it evolving? Wow. Um . . . it's not going anywhere. I mean, it is here to stay. People want cool products. People like to buy. Network marketers sell stuff. I think there will always be a market for meeting needs in the marketplace. And, with network marketing, it is simply cheaper and easier to bring stuff to people. So I see growth and longevity.

7

Sharing the Products and Opportunity

SPECIFICS ON HOW to share the products and opportunity with potential customers and business partners can vary from company to company. Many methods even vary from team to team within a particular company.

When you are getting started, have someone who is part of your upline take care of your initial presentations. When you invite in an outside expert to show the presentation, you will have a much higher success rate, especially with friends and family.

The most successful way to present the business or products to someone is still on a face-to-face level. Meeting in person always gets better results than sending someone to a conference call or web meeting. However, it is slightly more difficult to get people to meetings today than it was 10 or 15 years ago.

Having a full arsenal of ways to present the business and products is the best way to combat the subtle changes in our society.

Main Ways to Present the Business and Products

- One-on-one meetings
- Home meetings
- Hotel/conference center meetings
- Conference calls
- Web meetings
- Live streaming broadcasts

The easiest way to learn how to successfully run a meeting or present the opportunity is to go to a lot of meetings, especially in the beginning phase of your business. Even if you do not have a guest with you, your time will be well spent learning the ins and outs of presenting, how to set up for a presentation, and the best methods to wrap up a meeting with a strong call to action.

Three-Way Calls

The one skill that I can look back on and say without question made me the most money over the long term is three-way calling. Three-way calls can be successfully implemented before a presentation (during the invitation process), as a part of a presentation, and/or during the follow-up process.

The technical side of three-way calling can vary from phone to phone and carrier to carrier, so let's dig into how to have a successful three-way call.

The goal of a three-way call is to provide your potential business partner with a bigger picture of the business you are involved with, showing that you are not in business alone. Showing a potential business partner that you work with other successful entrepreneurs will go a long way toward establishing credibility for you and your new business.

You will want to have an updated biography from your sponsor or upline so that you can give them a proper introduction that will edify them and allow you to transfer your credibility.

Let's assume that you are on the phone with a potential business partner. The easiest way to do a three-way call is to simply say, "Hey, Joe, hang on a second," and then use the flash button and click over to call your upline or sponsor for the three-way call. I never ask for permission to do a three-way call.

When I dial my sponsor, I always clear the time and make sure he or she is available for a call. Then I give my sponsor a very quick rundown of the potential business partner who is on the line. Remember that all of this is happening in just a few seconds while the potential business partner is on the other line. After the quick rundown, I click back over to the main call, with my sponsor now on the line as well. Then I say, "Hey, Joe, it's actually your lucky day. That was the successful guy

I was telling you about earlier on the other line, and he had a couple of minutes to say hi." Joe (your potential business partner) will have no idea whether your upline/sponsor called you or you called your upline/sponsor—and it's not even important at this point because you are now all together.

Then I introduce my sponsor and tell Joe that he or she has only a couple of minutes to spend with us because of a busy schedule. I finish my introduction and edification and then turn the call over to my sponsor. Once I turn the call over, I never interrupt or offer any input. Interrupting your sponsor or upline in a three-way call is a good way to throw the credibility that you transferred right into the garbage. The credibility that you transfer from yourself to your sponsor is really the key to this whole process, because the job of the sponsor is not to explain all of the details or answer all of the questions; his or her job is to push the credibility right back to you. It is virtually impossible for you to sit on the phone with someone and tell him or her how great you are. Well, it isn't really impossible, but you will come off looking arrogant or worse. However, your upline can brag about you all day long, telling your potential business partner how lucky he or she is that you connected up and what a big business you are already putting together.

The transfer of credibility and the edification process are the magic behind three-way calls, and you will find that your potential business partner will listen to you in a different way once your sponsor/upline has told him or her how great you are!

The three-way call is also sometimes referred to as third-party validation, and many times it is just what a person needs to move on to the next step in the process. Consider making a list of leaders within your upline who are available for three-way calls; you can then work to pair up your potential business partners with the leader who might best relate to him or her.

8

Follow Up and Follow Through

STATISTICS SUGGEST THAT we simply do not follow up enough times to give ourselves a good chance to make a sale or bring on a new business partner. According to MarketingUK, 80 percent of sales occur after the fifth contact (www.marketinguk.co.uk/Marketing/80-of-sales-occur-after-the-5th-contact-but-most-business-owners-only-reach-out-to-new-leads-2-or-3-times.asp). People around the industry often say the fortune is in the follow-up, but I would make a small change to that saying and suggest that the fortune is lost in the follow up.

In addition to a traditional follow-up meeting, here are some methods that will help you stay in touch with your potential customers and business partners:

- **Send a short note** (yes, I am talking about snail mail). You might even consider finding a brochure or picture of a dream or goal that your potential business partner spoke about.
- **Leave a message.** Call your potential business partner during a time that it is unlikely he or she will pick up the phone and just leave a short message, saying that you were thinking about him or her.
- **Send an e-mail with an article or a special link.** Remember that people receive a lot of e-mail every single day. Put some thought into your follow-up e-mail and don't overdo it with a continuous flow of spam-like messages.
- **Invite the potential business partner to lunch or a dinner party.** This is a great way to get to know the person outside of business, and it shows that you are a real person with a life outside of your business. Whatever you do, do not invite someone to dinner and then have it turn into a business meeting.

A successful follow-up is one that you do! Just stay in touch with people and serve them, whether or not they join you in business or as a customer.

Handling Follow-Up Objections

Here are the four most common objections you will hear and some simple responses:

Objection #1: "I don't have time."

Response: "I understand you are busy. As a matter of fact, that's why I thought of you. I want to show you a way to get some of your time back by leveraging technology and social media. Let's sit down for a cup of coffee. I'll run some numbers by you. If you like what you see, we can move forward; if not, no big deal."

Objection #2: "I don't have the money."

Response: "I understand that. That's why I thought of you. And frankly, I'm not after your money. The money is the easy part. My goal is to help you make more than $1,000 in your first month so that you won't have to worry about start-up costs. Let's sit down for a cup of coffee. I'll run some numbers by you. If you like what you see, we can move forward; if not, no big deal."

Objection #3: "I tried something like this before, and it didn't work for me."

Response: "Let me ask you a really simple question. Would you want to marry every single person you ever dated? Of course not, right? In fact, you probably had some bad experiences, but that didn't stop you from looking until you found the right one. Listen, explaining the differences are easy. Let's sit down for a cup of coffee. I'll run some numbers by you. If you like what you see, we can move forward; if not, no big deal."

Objection #4: "I'm not the salesperson type."

Response: "I am so glad you said that, because I found that salespeople don't tend to do as well as people who aren't salespeople at all. But I am happy to go over exactly how we are leveraging social media to do the heavy lifting. Let's sit down for a cup of coffee. I'll run some numbers by you. If you like what you see, we can move forward; if not, no big deal."

9

Leadership
The Difference Maker

TEAMS RISE AND fall based on leadership, so let's look at six attributes of a network marketing leader with some quotes that I found from famous leaders from all walks of life:

1. *Positive Attitude:* "Ability is what you're capable of doing. Motivation determines what you do. Attitude determines how well you do it." —Lou Holtz
2. *Character:* "People grow through experience if they meet life honestly and courageously. This is how character is built." —Eleanor Roosevelt
3. *Consistency:* "In baseball, my theory is to strive for consistency, not to worry about the numbers. If you dwell on statistics you get shortsighted; if you aim for consistency, the numbers will be there at the end." —Tom Seaver
4. *Vision:* "Good business leaders create a vision, articulate the vision, passionately own the vision, and relentlessly drive it to completion." —Jack Welch
5. *Confidence:* "To be a great champion you must believe you are the best. If you're not, pretend you are." —Muhammad Ali
6. *Commitment:* "The quality of a person's life is in direct proportion to their commitment to excellence, regardless of their chosen field of endeavor." —Vince Lombardi

The person who has had the most impact on my life as a leader is Bo Short. Bo has written two books on the subject of leadership and has spoken around the world to more than 1 million people on the subject. Bo also set a record for growth at the Shaklee Corporation for the fastest team to reach the Master Coordinator level in the 55-year history of the company. I was honored to talk with Bo about leadership and the network marketing industry:

Ty Tribble: You have been a leader in the network marketing industry for more than 20 years. What is the one characteristic that every leader should possess?

Bo Short: As president of the American Leadership Foundation, and having been blessed to have interviewed so many great leaders in my life, I would suggest that the core characteristics of leadership are vision, courage, perseverance, responsibility, and character. From those spring all of the other important attributes, such as kindness, risk, tact, teamwork, empathy, and so on. However, at the heart of leadership, I would suggest that vision and character are paramount. They act as a force multiplier to fuel a leader's direction.

Ty Tribble: How important is having a dream and vision to the success of the newest network marketer?

Bo Short: Without question, it is the vital starting point. This attribute offers hope to the new network marketer. Hope is the heartbeat of action. Vision gives one the ability to look forward and live out of one's imagination, versus looking backward and reliving one's failures. It need not be a big dream but one that incites the individual to take one step farther each day.

I also think it is important to point out that if one does not know what he or she wants, then what that person does not want becomes a cause for action. Some people do not begin the process running toward something but rather running away from something. Either way is fine, as it moves them in the right direction. For the person who doesn't know what they want, it is only a matter of time until they find what they do want and then focus on that.

Ty Tribble: What kind of impact can leadership have on a network marketing organization?

Bo Short: I believe there are two areas, beyond effort, that are essential in developing a growing, cohesive team. One is people skills, and the other, leadership development. The ability to inspire others to do things they may not normally do is critical if one is to develop a large network. This ability to influence proper behavior is essential to large-scale duplication. Poor leadership can have the opposite effect. Accelerated growth depends on one's ability to lead effectively.

Ty Tribble: How do you help your aspiring leaders become better at leading?

Bo Short: Personal counseling, promoting the reading of books that offer direction and inspiration, and the constant understanding that people do what I do, not what I say to do.

In regard to books, sales give financial depth to an organization, but books give depth to the leaders of the organization. Books give the prospective leaders insight into the process and the challenges and failures of those who have ultimately persevered and won.

Personal mentoring allows me to help assist and cultivate the development of an individual at his or her own rate. Everyone needs something different at different times. Personally mentoring people allows me the ability to fill that need.

Last, an understanding that what I say pales in comparison to what I do. People have learned to look beyond the words and into the action of so-called leaders. Therefore, it is incumbent upon us to live the words we use.

Ty Tribble: You wrote two books on leadership and studied many great leaders. Who is your all-time favorite leader and why?

Bo Short: Without question, I believe that George Washington was the greatest leader. While far from perfect, as we all are, he was a visionary who came to understand his perspective role in history and accepted it. During a critical time during our country's founding, he felt very insignificant. He had troops who were starving, freezing, and most unpaid. His soldiers were fighting less for the country and more for their colonies. It was at this moment that George Washington walked among his troops and said, "Let only Americans stand watch this night." What may have, at that moment, appeared insignificant proved later to give breath to the Declaration of Independence.

Leadership can be lonely and oftentimes is. Leaders can feel very insignificant. However, what they do *then* is what matters. George Washington's vision, courage, perseverance, responsibility, and character helped establish a country and gave flight to the American experiment.

Ty Tribble: Who has had the greatest impact on your life as a leader?

Bo Short: Different people for different reasons. My dad gave me a clear understanding that anything was possible and that success was a result of consistent effort over time. Nothing was instant, but I controlled myself and my own willingness to work.

My mom gave me the blessing of kindness and empathy. She always saw the possibilities in people and spoke to them in a way that allowed them to be better than they may actually be. She elevated people.

My wife, Sandy, was and has always been my inspiration. At the writing of this book, we are celebrating 30 years of marriage. She has always believed in me and accepted nothing from me but my very best effort. Most of what I have accomplished would not have been possible without Sandy's focus, determination, and belief in me.

Ty Tribble: What leadership book do you recommend for an aspiring leader?

Bo Short: Wow. That is a tough one. I love books. There are different books for different reasons. However, if I was forced to recommend one it would be *The Arc of Ambition: Defining the Leadership Journey*, by James Champy and Nitin Nohria.

Ty Tribble: You are one of the few leaders in the industry who maintains a balance of online and offline marketing. Talk about the importance of the Internet along with maintaining the offline presence.

Bo Short: One can easily put his or her head in the sand and pretend technology does not exist. Or, one can embrace the possibilities that technology offers us. I choose the latter.

The ability to utilize the Internet serves only to put more arrows in one's quiver. It offers a builder the opportunity to reach farther and faster, thus expediting his or her success. It also gives one the ability to be located in a city and work in countless cities in one night.

However, a sustainable business is still built on relationships and therefore requires more than online activity. Using the Internet properly does not interfere with the relationship-building process. It only adds to it. Really knowing your team is personal and requires a personal relationship.

Ty Tribble: Share some words of encouragement with the newest person learning about the industry and those who are looking to rekindle their businesses.

Bo Short: Success in this industry is a result of doing enough of the right things. Superhuman strength is not needed. Your best and highest effort is. Let me say that again: Your best and highest effort, coupled with doing enough of the right things, is all that is needed to win.

You can accomplish anything that you set your mind and heart on. You, however, will be your biggest critic. You must learn to speak to yourself in an encouraging manner. You must realize that your best lays ahead of you. You were not put on this earth to get by. You were put here to be significant.

You will positively affect the lives of thousands of people by what you do each day. Become better each day. I am proud of each and every one of you. Always lead.

PART

III

The Internet Changes Everything

10

Attraction Marketing

MANY OF THE most successful network marketers today who utilize the Internet have the "attraction" model at the center of everything they do online. Whether they are posting something to their blog, tweeting a message on Twitter, or updating their Facebook wall, every action is meant to attract and influence potential business partners and customers.

My good friend Ann Sieg boils attraction marketing down to two words: teaching sells. Ann first learned of the concept by accident when she went to see a speaker demonstrate at a health awareness seminar. The seminar was basically an educational class that showed people how to improve their health and their diet without buying anything.

The presenter first talked about the body's different systems and how they worked; then she gave a visual demonstration of how the digestive system works, using a nylon stocking to represent the human colon.

Ann describes the presenter getting "geared up" in her apron and latex gloves and then beginning to stuff food from the average American diet into the nylon, which represented the large intestine. First went a hamburger, next french fries, then a can's worth of chili, a jelly doughnut, 12 ounces of Coca-Cola, and finally a milkshake. Right away, the nylon stocking became clogged as the food stuck together. To move the food to the bottom of the nylon, the presenter had to work hard, kneading the food down the nylon with her hands.

Needless to say, the demonstration was not pretty and scared many attendees into giving up fast food forever.

Then the presenter grabbed a fresh nylon stocking and began to dump in apple slices, grapes, pineapple chunks, celery, carrots, and other fruits and vegetables. The fruits and vegetables slid right down the nylon stocking without any prodding by the presenter.

At the end of the presentation, the woman simply mentioned that the products she had could help with some of these issues like improving digestions. That's it. No big sales pitch, no high-pressure close—just high-quality information with an offer to act on what was taught.

Attending this presentation was a breakthrough moment for Ann, who began to implement the technique into her own business. Sales began to pour in, and Ann began to do these health seminars throughout her local area, even for other teams outside of her own.

Then something even crazier began to happen. Ann began receiving unsolicited calls from people who heard about her presentations from others who had attended. This seems like a simple little thing, but at the time, very few people in the industry of network marketing were getting unsolicited referrals.

Ann was excited about her breakthrough and quickly went from selling a few hundred dollars per month to regularly selling more than $3,000 of products every month.

This example of offline attraction is really no different than online attraction marketing. Ann was giving valuable content and instruction in the form of her health seminars. Without any sales pitch, people were buying Ann's health products because they found real value in the information and learned that the product actually solved a problem.

Selling is very easy when you have something that others want, need, or desire. In 2006, my wife and I owned a business that sold products on eBay.

The year 2006 happened to be the tenth anniversary of Tickle Me Elmo, a doll that would giggle when tickled and that had been a huge fad. That year, Fisher-Price released TMX, or Tickle Me Elmo Ten. Demand for TMX was extreme, with stores selling out of the crazy and secretive doll that was packaged in such a way that you couldn't even see the entire doll. As luck would have it, my wife and I had purchased 30 TMX dolls from Costco on the day they arrived. We held onto them as stores ran out and then began to slowly list them one by one on eBay. Our average sales price for the doll that cost us about $30 was over $100.

People wanted the new TMX, and we had them in stock, ready for Christmas. Selling the TMX doll was easy; in fact, there was virtually no selling involved whatsoever. We listed TMX in one-day auctions, and people went nuts bidding. We had what people wanted, and people lined up to get it, paying a premium.

Attraction is not about finding the Tickle Me Elmos of the world. It is more about finding a need in the marketplace and filling it.

Ann Sieg's story doesn't end with her health seminars. Ann later went on to write *The 7 Great Lies of Network Marketing* and *The Renegade Network Marketer*. Ann's books have been downloaded by more than 350,000 people, and her savvy marketing has helped build a family company (80/20) into a $10 million online empire.

Ann saw a need in the network marketing industry for some straight talk about selling and marketing, especially online. Her controversial *7 Great Lies* book tapped into the feelings many people had about the industry and caused a firestorm among several leaders who felt threatened or even targeted.

From a purely marketing perspective, Ann's *7 Great Lies* was a work of genius. If someone hated the book, they voiced their concern over what they called a horrible book and person, which got more people talking about it and downloading it to see what the controversy was all about. Those who liked

the book promoted it as well. Either way, Ann got people talking, which, in turn, helped build her a large list of network
marketers that eventually turned into a $10 million business.

The *7 Great Lies* content that Ann created was a simple
eBook that she gave away for free. The *7 Great Lies* ebook outlined the problem that many people were facing in the network marketing industry at the time. Then Ann positioned
her *Renegade Network Marketer* ebook as the solution to the
problems outlined and promptly sold tens of thousands of copies for $60 each.

Ty Tribble: Tell me about the early days and your initial experience with the industry of network marketing.

Ann Sieg: I started network marketing or more so direct sales
more than 24 years ago when I was pregnant with my second
child. This company is world renowned for its cosmetic line
and pink Cadillacs.

We were of very humble means at that time. I was a
gymnastics coach, and my husband had just entered the
banking industry. I wanted to bring additional income into
our family household and had a big dream of buying our
first home through that opportunity.

I did numerous facials and home parties and ended up
giving up on it about a year and a half later. I was still
coaching and had two little boys to raise with another one
on the way.

I was glad for the experience. I went on to do a number
of different home party plans and even Avon (which I
really loved).

I always tried to integrate my family into what I was
doing. For example, my two younger boys learned to put on
the labels and bag my catalogs. I had them go around the

neighborhood with me while I knocked on doors. "Ding, dong, Avon calling."

I really enjoy sales tremendously. It wasn't until 2002 that I got into network marketing at a much more serious level. I wanted to reach the six-figure income they talked about. That put me on a whole new journey of discovery.

Ty Tribble: How did you balance business and family life?

Ann Sieg: Well, my boys are all raised now, so it's not as big of an issue. But back 10 years ago, I was homeschooling my two boys, helping run my husband's windshield replacement business, and managing our real estate investments.

It was very hectic, but the way I stay ahead of that is planning. I set aside time to structure out just about everything I can. I don't like to do things in a helter-skelter fashion. I am very systems minded.

I learned most of this from my mother, who was a teacher. She always planned things out the night before and kept very tight to-do lists. I'm pretty much the same way.

The other thing is I incorporated all our activities as a family. Not segmented activities. When my boys were in traditional schooling, it wasn't uncommon for me to be running 10 to 12 different activities through our church and school. I demonstrated to them that I was a very involved active mother, and as a result, all three of our sons worked within our various family businesses.

I firmly believe project management is an essential skill in running a business and organization.

Ty Tribble: What kind of obstacles did you run up against while building your business?

Ann Sieg: Probably the biggest obstacle was getting my team to do what I would do. And second, I ran out of qualified prospects to talk to. This was back in 2004, when I had done everything my company and upline told me to do and then some.

Aside from that, I see business as a series of problem-solving exercises. It is my mind-set or perception of any challenges that makes a huge difference. I don't see obstacles as an end-of-the-road situation, but more so another test of figuring things out and trying new methods—hence the name Renegade—the ability to think outside the box.

Ty Tribble: You run a family business. Tell us how your family participates in your business.

Ann Sieg: My husband is the CFO [chief financial officer] and my eldest son is our marketing director. I am the CEO [chief executive officer]. Our business began with me and my willingness to go in and get the job done. As my family saw my successes, they saw the opportunity for us to incorporate and take our business to the next level.

At one time my middle son was our shipping manager and my youngest son was our Pay-Per-Click (Google Advertising) optimization expert. Currently neither one of them works in my business, but I am open to them joining me again someday. The challenge is they would have to really take the time to learn and understand my industry. I don't think that is going to happen. My eldest son, on the other hand, is very much my business partner and master-mind collaborator.

We have a lot of fun together, and we work very hard.

Ty Tribble: What is your biggest piece of advice for a mom who is just getting started?

Ann Sieg: Be aware of the family economy. Everyone contributes in different ways. It is important to train your children to see how they can contribute to the family dynamic.

Set proper expectations. Life is a series of agreements and definitely holds true in the family.

"You do this and I'll do that." Train them to fill their end of the bargain. Business is the same.

I do not like a family model where the children are catered to left and right and are not taught to take on higher levels of responsibility. Children are far more capable than we give them credit. They are smart and adaptable. Give them room to grow, and they'll make it happen.

Ty Tribble: We have been friends for many years, and one of the things that I admire about you is your ability to adapt to changes in technology and trends while maintaining a focus on business basics like real marketing. Can you talk about your influences, such as books, training materials, and mentors?

Ann Sieg: Thank you so much for the compliment.

High-quality team members have helped me adapt to technology and trends. I like the Henry Ford management model of having experts at the tip of my fingers.

Aside from that is my own mind-set, which is to always be looking ahead for what's next, commonly called a fore-runner or early adapter.

My father taught me to think for myself. I'm grateful for that.

I read constantly from a variety of authors. As far as marketing, I learned directly from John Carlton and David Garfinkel. I've studied from Dan Kennedy, Perry Marshall, Frank Kern, and Gary Halbert.

When it comes to business, I would say the biggest influence was Eben Pagan through his Get Altitude conference. I also read from business authors on a regular basis and interview them for my Leaders' Circle membership.

I've interviewed Guy Kawasaki, Perry Marshall, David Garfinkel, Daniel Coyle, Simon Sinek, Ari Weinzweig (really like him), and several other authors.

I find that by studying authors, trainers, and educators outside the network marketing industry, I remain fresh and innovative in my marketing and leadership.

Ty Tribble: What type of impact does the economy have on an industry like network marketing? Is there any advice you can give to help people deal with the current economic climate?

Ann Sieg: I think the economy has a huge impact on our industry. I have seen a change in what price points people will tolerate along with the challenge of closing a sale. At the same time, that increases the need for people to improve even more on their marketing and salesmanship. I think that's a good thing!

I've mentioned in a few of my team meetings that it's not 2007 anymore. It's an entirely different climate than it was five years ago.

According to Gallup there is a shortage of more than 1 billion jobs around the world. As a result there will be millions of people coming our way looking for new ways to make money. Personally I believe more millionaires will be created over the next three to five years of network marketing than in the past 50 years combined.

The key is to be ready and positioned as they come our way. I am a strong believer that the biggest asset you build is yourself. You do that by developing skill sets that have value in the marketplace, not just becoming a billboard for your network marketing opportunity.

People sponsor-shop, and they want the best sponsor possible. Your ability to lead people is paramount. That begins by showing up in your business on a daily basis and leading yourself first.

Last, I am about finding a hungry targeted audience, but what I want even more is a hungry audience with money. I have a whole series of videos on my Facebook Fan Page that describes where that money can be found. I call it the Triple Dippers. Position yourself in front of this audience; get them to know, like, and trust you; and you should do just fine. This particular audience has very high and discriminating standards—all the more reason for people to develop business professionalism.

Ty Tribble: What are you working on right now? What are you excited about?

Ann Sieg: I have formed a marketing team once again and am in big team-building mode. My reason for doing so is that with all the changes going on, I felt it necessary, as an industry leader, to get back in the trenches and find out what works and what doesn't work.

We got going in June, and I have to say I am very happy we made that decision. Building teams is one of my biggest strengths. It is a fairly natural skill set from having raised a family along with coaching in the sports world for 15 years.

In addition to testing and maximizing our marketing efforts, I've been able to reach #2 in my primary company in five short months.

My favorite part of team building is masterminding and collaborating with team members to make everything work even better.

11

Funded Proposals and
Marketing Funnels

THE MODEL OF giving away something of value for free, and then selling something on the back end is called *funnel marketing*, and some might consider it part of an overall strategy called a *funded proposal*. There are few online marketing trends that rival the impact that the funded proposal concept has made on the network marketing industry.

The network marketing funded proposal concept was pioneered by Joe Schroeder but was really brought to the masses by my friend and founder of Magnetic Sponsoring, Mike Dillard.

Today, Mike is considered by many to be the leading force in bringing online marketing to network marketers. More than 300,000 people have subscribed to his video boot camp/newsletter, and he earned $7 million online in less than three years. Mike is also the creator of BetterNetworker.com, the largest social network and community dedicated to the network marketing profession.

But Mike will be the first to tell you that he was not an overnight success; he spent his first six years in the industry struggling, racking up credit card debt, and pawning his possessions just to eat. After learning about the funded proposal concept, Mike went from waiting tables to being a millionaire in less than 18 months.

Funded proposals typically consist of giving away something of value (a newsletter, seven-day video boot camp, or ebook) for free in exchange for a person's contact information, usually name and e-mail address. Once the name and e-mail address is collected, the information is placed into an e-mail autoresponder that begins the process of selling a low-ticket information product (usually some type of training materials). When a customer purchases the low-ticket product, he or she is approached in a consultative manner about working with the creator or affiliate of the funded proposal.

In a sense, the funded proposal concept flips the funnel when it comes to recruiting people for a business. The approach is not "Are you interested in making more money?"; you already know this to be true based on the product that the customer just purchased. The approach is more along the lines of "How can we work together to accomplish your goals?"

A funded proposal can be created on your own, or you can use one that has already been created, such as Mike Dillard's *Magnetic Sponsoring* or Ann Sieg's *Renegade Network Marketer*. The only issue you might face with using someone else's funded proposal is that there is a marketing life span on these types of programs.

Ann Sieg and I recently collaborated on a funded proposal called MLM Blog Secrets. In MLM Blog Secrets, we gave away more than three hours of video training (Blogging for Prospects) on the art and science of blogging for the network marketing industry. The low-ticket item was the MLM Blog Secrets product that goes through the basics of blogging; then we offered an up-sell of a higher-ticket product called MLM Blog Code, which provided more advanced training on the subject of blogging for network marketers. The reason this collaboration worked so well is that I was able to offer Ann some fresh training on the subject of blogging and she could approach her list and networkers online with a new marketing funnel that would attract people she may not have attracted in the past.

A funded proposal is usually part of an overall marketing funnel. When creating your own marketing funnel, I find it most effective to start with the end.

What is the goal of the funnel? Starting with something other than the end creates a huge number of mistakes in strategy that can be very costly in the long run. For example, I see a number of blogs created by network marketers who have advertising from Google (called Google AdSense) on them. If your goal is to find customers and business partners for your network marketing business so that you can create residual income and achieve the dreams that you have listed in your dream notebook, it makes absolutely no sense to post ads on your blog that promote someone else's business opportunity. In addition to the prospect of losing your potential business partner or customer to someone else's ad on your own blog, the profitability of Google AdSense is nothing like it once was.

So you want to start with the end result you are looking for and work your way backward to create a marketing funnel for your business.

Let's say my goal is to create new customers for my weight loss products. Here are the basics of the marketing funnel that I would be working to create:

Goal: Find customers interested in weight loss.

· The end of the funnel would be an order placed for a weight loss package, thus creating your new customer. This is not the true end of the funnel, but I would describe it as the end of the beginning. You will want to make additional offers and specials to your existing customers down the road.

Next we need to consider the sales process or what makes a person buy. Obviously a person buys a weight loss package because he or she wants to lose weight, but what things usually take place before someone pulls the trigger and makes the purchase. This is where you will need to do some research. I have never created a weight loss funnel myself, but my educated guess would be that people make a weight loss purchase when they see results from someone they know or relate to. So I know that testimonials and before and after pictures will be a big part of the funnel.

According to a Gallup Poll,[1] nearly 6 in 10 Americans want to lose weight, so finding target customers should not be difficult. The question then becomes, what do you use to grab their attention and attract the people who want to lose weight to your funnel?

The answer is offering either information or samples. The information might be a helpful ebook on the secrets of weight loss, and the samples might be a free weight loss shake or protein bar. Now that we have gone through what is included in the funnel, beginning with the end result, let's take a walk through the funnel from the start so that you can get a better understanding of how everything fits together.

The funnel begins with a free sample, free report, or free ebook offer. The offer would be located on what is called a lead capture page or squeeze page, and the sole purpose of the free offer is to capture a person's name and e-mail address, thereby putting that person in your funnel.

Once you have the potential customer in your funnel, you can begin the sales process. This is usually done using an e-mail autoresponder. An e-mail autoresponder allows you to create specific e-mail messages and send them to your potential customers at a chosen date and time. In our weight loss example, the e-mail campaign can be as simple as telling the story of others who have had success with the program. Before and after pictures, video testimonials, and personal written stories from people will do the selling for you. You could write a thousand-word essay about your product, complete with significant scientific support, but it would pale in comparison to a one-minute video that includes before and after pictures from someone who weighed 220 pounds before purchasing the weight loss program and now weighs 185 pounds.

---

[1] www.gallup.com/poll/21859/close-americans-want-lose-weight.aspx

Testimonials and stories always sell better than facts and science. After including the weight loss success stories in your e-mails, all you need to do is point people to the order page so that they can experience the same thing that others have experienced.

The one missing element to this funnel is people. You need people to visit your page in the first place so that they can enter their information and download the free report or request the free sample. Generating traffic is an integral part of any online marketing campaign, and the good news is that there are lots of great ways to do it in today's Internet world.

To grab a free bonus live interview that I did with Mike Dillard, visit www.TyTribble.com/MikeDillardInterview.

12

Generating Visitors and Site Traffic

THE SKILL THAT seems to elude many Internet marketers is the ability to generate traffic online. You can have the greatest opportunity in the world with the most amazing products and your marketing funnel can be optimized and running like a fine-tuned machine, but without traffic, the whole operation will be worthless.

We're going to focus on a number of proven techniques to generate highly targeted traffic so that the leads you create with your marketing funnel will be the most qualified prospects for your business and/or products.

Pay-per-Click Advertising

Google AdWords (pay per click) are best described as the small ads that you see when you search for something on Google. When I first used Google AdWords in January 2003, I thought that I found the Holy Grail. At the time, I set my budget at $10 per day and my average cost per click was about five cents. I hadn't found a network marketer who used Google AdWords earlier, so the competition was virtually nonexistent.

For example, back in 2003, I could place an ad on Google for the search term "network marketing" and for the number one position; I would pay roughly five cents each time a person clicked on my ad. Today, if you place an ad for "network marketing," you would pay roughly $2 per click for the number-one position.

Unless you know precisely what you are doing and your ad is extremely targeted, Google AdWords is not a viable option for driving traffic.

Facebook and LinkedIn also have pay-per-click advertising in place that might be better suited for the network marketer, but I wouldn't go near it without hiring an expert to put together and optimize the campaigns. The money you spend having your campaigns optimized by a true expert will be saved over and over when you consider the costs of trial and error.

Free Traffic Methods

Blog Comments

Placing thoughtful comments on blogs within your niche while making sure that you enter your website information is a great way to gain valuable traffic. In Chapter 13, I suggest reading five blog posts each day, which would allow you to kill two birds with one stone: gaining valuable knowledge from reading the blog and leaving a comment on each of them.

When you thoughtfully comment on a blog post within your niche, people may be curious about who you are and then decide to visit your site. An effective comment might look something like this:

> Great point, Miss Blog Author. I love what you said about (specifics related to the topic). As a matter of fact, I recently wrote about (specifics) as well. I agree with what you said about (specifics) but see this (specifics) a little but differently. Love to get your opinion. . . .

I never leave a link within the comment section; I always just place my link in the spot for website. Letting the author know what you think specifically about his or her blog post and inviting that person to check out your opposing viewpoint is a good way to not only get the author to read your blog but also get the author's readers to see what you have to say. Subtlety should be the rule when commenting on blogs.

Forum Comments

Being an active and thoughtful participant in an online forum is another way to drive traffic to your blog. Forums are another place where you can learn more about your niche market. Being an active participant does not mean getting caught up in forum drama while spending hours a day waiting for people to respond to your witty forums threads.

Five Tips That Will Help You Market on Forums

1. Take your eyes off of yourself and focus on helping others.
2. Do not promote your links anywhere outside of your signature line. Most forums have rules to follow, and many of them allow you to post your links in a signature line. An example signature might be: Warmest - Ty Tribble I help people make "6 figures on Facebook in 12 Months" Link the "6 figures on Facebook" to your presentation page and otherwise go about your business. If someone asks about it, respond but don't jump down anybody's throat.
3. Your objective is to offer advice on subjects you know about and answer questions that you have the answers to, but be careful not to come across as someone who has every answer. Your secondary objective is to learn from others on the site. Gain knowledge that you might be able to share with your team in the future.
4. You don't want to be a time-wasting regular, but you do want to be known. Forums can be a massive time waster, so be very careful and make sure you use your time wisely. Drop in once a day for a couple of minutes, make a post, and then move on to other productive activities.
5. Don't waste your time with forums that have little traffic. Some high-traffic forums include RichDad, BetterNetworker, WAHM, and the Warrior Forum.

Article Marketing

Article marketing is similar to blogging in a lot of ways, and I am an advocate of taking a blog article and repurposing it into an article that I would then submit to article directories. Most people agree that content is still king online, and the more unique and interesting content you can have about your niche online, the better.

Before you write a batch of articles, make sure to study the format of articles that you find within your niche. Also make sure to spend some time with Google's keyword tool. The keyword tool will help you focus your efforts and place keywords in your articles that will pay off in the long run.

Current Top 10 Sites (Based on Traffic) to Submit Your Articles

1. Knol.google.com
2. eHow.com
3. Squidoo.com
4. Ezinearticles.com
5. Hubpages.com
6. Examiner.com
7. Articlebase.com
8. Technorati.com
9. Seekingalpha.com
10. Voices.Yahoo.com

Several of the top 10 article sites are "no follow," meaning linking from the site offers no influence in the search engine results; however, you might still see tremendous traffic directly from the site or once the search engines pick up your article. In other words, you might not see any added influence on your blog by linking to it from the article, but the search engines might find the article and you will gain traffic in that manner.

Press Releases

Press releases are another way to generate traffic to a website, and the impact of a press release can be far greater than the few days when the press actually pick up the news release. One of the greatest benefits of doing a press release is the search engine traction that you get by landing your business on these highly ranked news sites.

You might consider putting out a press release when you launch a new website because the incoming links to your site from the highly ranked news and syndicated content sites will help with your own search results.

There are some free press release submission sites, but I found that you pretty much get what you pay for. You're looking for results, and finding one new business partner will (in most cases) easily pay for the money you spend on the release. As far as paid press releases go, I've used Marketwire and PRWeb in the past, and both have shown to be reputable.

When it comes to writing your press release, it is a good idea to have a look at some of the press releases available online to get a better understanding of the format. Press releases tend to be written a bit differently than a blog post or article. You want to stand out, but you also want to make sure that as many sites pick up your release as possible.

When writing your press release, remember that it should be more along the lines of a news story in lieu of a sales pitch, but at the same time, you also want to grab attention. The goal of a press release is to get the reader to visit your website or con-tact you directly, so you don't want to give up all of the details of your site or project in the release itself. You want to tease the reader with content appetizers while leaving the main course on your site.

Writing a press release is a daunting task for most people, so you might consider finding someone to write it for you. Elance.com and Freelancer.com are good places to find free-lancers who will write your press release for a fee.

Things to Consider Promoting via a Press Release

- Launching a new blog or website
- Launching a new product
- Announcing new additions to your team
- Promoting your meetings

One special note about announcing new additions to your team: this can be a great way to show the world that your team is growing and also make your new business partners feel like a million dollars by including a promotional biography.

Remember to repost your press releases on Facebook, Twitter, and LinkedIn to get maximum exposure.

13

Blogging for Prospects

In OCTOBER 2003, I launched MLMBlog.net, the first weblog with content related to the network marketing industry as a whole. At the time, there were a handful of blogs related to specific companies, most of them skewed toward bad personal experiences. When I launched MLMBlog.net, I had no real goal of creating a site that attracted thousands of daily visitors or a site that would dominate the search engines for important industry keywords. In fact, my first goal was simply to see if I could get someone to read what I wrote. I figured that if I could get one person to read my blog, I might have a chance to relate to that person and perhaps we would share something in common.

Using a blog for business was a complete shot in the dark for a couple of reasons. First, early bloggers generally seemed to frown upon blogging for business and utilizing advertising. Second, no one had really figured out how to turn blog visitors into customers.

There is still a very fine line between providing readers with quality content and promoting a business.

There should be no secret that in today's day and age, having a web presence is an absolute necessity. I believe that setting up a blog is the easiest way to get up and running online in a professional manner for very little cost.

People tend to feel a higher level of trust when reading a blog versus browsing a website. My son Tyler (10 years old at the time) would occasionally watch Internet marketing training videos with me; one day, I heard a noise from my office and found him with a whiteboard and marker pen, drawing out and narrating an Internet marketing technique that we had watched on video a couple of days earlier. Many people seem to feel overwhelmed and lost when it comes to blogging, or anything else related to Internet marketing, and I thought that if I could get my 10-year-old son to do a video training on the subject of blogging, people would generally feel more at ease and more likely to think that they could figure it out.

About that time, I was working on a product called MLM Blog Secrets, a training program to help the newest person launch a blog, create blog articles, and drive traffic to the blog. So Tyler and I set out to create a fun video where he and I would teach a blogging strategy. First, Tyler and I hopped in our Porsche and took a trip to get a haircut and a hot towel treatment so that he would look ready for his Internet marketing video debut. Once Tyler was ready, he delivered an amazing five-minute presentation on a marketing strategy called the triangle of trust.

The triangle of trust was a technique that we had learned from Internet marketing legend Frank Kern. Picture three points on a triangle, with one point being a video, one point being a blog post, and the last point being a sales page or offer. Kern talks about utilizing a video to attract people to your blog post, where you can then direct people to the product or business you are looking to sell. When Tyler presented the strategy, he said something that was very profound for a 10-year-old, something that Kern doesn't mention in his video.

Tyler said that people trust blogs over websites because when people go to a blog, they are usually looking for information. When a people go to websites, they are usually going to buy something.

So given a choice to have a web developer create a website that only he or she can update with new information, I would suggest you have someone develop you a blog that you can learn to update on your own, quickly and easily for free.

Not All Blogs Are Created Equal

When I say that not all blogs are created equal, what I am really referring to is the blogging platform that a blog is created on. There are many ways to create a blog, but few of them give you the control, updates, and bells and whistles that you need if you plan on blogging over the long term for your business.

Many people initially use Blogger/Blogspot or WordPress .com when they start blogging because they are free and easy to set up. But the best place for your blog is a web host using the WordPress.org format.

The easiest way for me to explain the difference is that Blogger/Blogspot and WordPress.com are hosted sites where someone else has the final say about your content and blog, much like renting a house. Let's say you are renting a home and decide to do some improvements. You paint the inside and outside, you replace the kitchen countertops, and you remodel the bathroom, only to learn that your landlord has decided to not allow you to rent the place after your lease expires. All of the hard work and money that you put into the rental house is now going down the drain because you didn't own the property. That is much like hosting your blog on Blogger or WordPress.com. You do not own the real estate, so Blogger or WordPress.com can (and have done so many times in the past) shut down your blog at any time.

If you find your own host and upload WordPress.org on your own domain, you are in an ownership position. You own the content and your domain, along with the search engine status that you have accumulated over time.

Examples of web hosts that make it very easy to set up your own blog include GoDaddy.com (also a domain seller), Dreamhost, and AmeriNOC. I have used all three in the past and have had the best service and reliability from AmeriNOC. You can get hosting from AmeriNOC for less than $5 per month.

Once you get your hosting, you'll need a domain name. You can acquire a domain name through AmeriNOC for less than $10 per year or at GoDaddy.com for just under $12 per year. I recommend using your name for your first blog. My personal blog is located at TyTribble.com. As you grow your business, people will inevitably search for you in a search engine such as Google, Yahoo!, or Bing. You want your main site to come up as the number one search result on all search engines, and using your name in the domain will help with that. I also suggest that people use .com domains whenever possible. If your name is not available as a .com domain, you might consider something like workwith(yourname).com or (yourname)blog.com.

Once you have your domain and hosting, you are ready to set up your blog. The process is relatively simple, and a quick search of "how to set up a wordpress.org blog" on YouTube will provide you with several instructional videos. If you decided to work with AmeriNOC as your host, a representative will help you with the process should you get stuck anywhere.

After you have WordPress.org uploaded, you have a decision to make about the look and feel of your site. You can find a free theme, pay for a premium blog theme, or hire someone to create the blog of your dreams.

If you decide to choose a free theme, there are hundreds to choose from.

Free Theme Suggestions

- Intrepidity
- Platform

- Organic theme
- zeeReputation

You can change your themes and see what they look like in the WordPress back office right sidebar under "appearance."

A word of warning: Many people tend to choose themes that they are attracted to from a color perspective. If you are planning on using your blog for marketing your business, I suggest finding a theme that has less color and more white space. You want the reader to focus on your content, not the fancy moving pictures and bright colors.

Going with the free theme option is what I did for a long time, but I found myself spending a lot of time playing around with my theme instead of creating content for my blog that would attract more readers.

The second option is to choose a premium paid theme. Under most circumstances, a premium theme will provide you with more options.

Companies That Provide Quality Paid Themes

- MLM Blog Theme (a theme specifically designed with the network marketer in mind)
- WooThemes
- ElegantThemes
- ThemeForest

Remember that a paid theme is still a theme that may need some tweaking to fit your needs. Just because you pay for the theme does not mean it will be perfect out of the box.

The last option is to have someone design a theme for you. This is the option that I recommend for most people. The money is well spent and can be recouped in a hurry because your time is freed up, allowing you to focus on creating great content and driving traffic to your blog instead of learning HTML in order to fine-tune and tweak your site.

The design team that I have used most recently to overhaul MLMBlog.net and create a brand-new TyTribble.com is Wordpress Makeover. Rick Robbins is an amazing artist, and he understands the goals of an Internet network marketer, a very rare combination of talents.

After your blog is dialed in, you will need to shift gears and focus on creating high-quality content that will attract readers.

Creating High-Quality Blog Content

The first thing I suggest that new aspiring bloggers do is to start reading other blogs. I recommend reading five blog posts per day that revolve around the niche topic that you plan to blog about. One of the beautiful things about the human mind is our ability to take in information and process that information in a unique manner. If you read five blog posts a day, there is very little chance that anyone else in the world will have read the same five blog posts in the order you read them.

After reading the five posts, I recommend taking a paragraph from your favorite blog post and creating your own post around that paragraph. I call this exercise drafting off of thought leaders. Once you paste the paragraph into the editor of your own blog, write a sentence about why you liked that particular blog post and then write a second sentence about why you like the author. Next, link to the original blog post, giving full credit, add a picture that best represents the post, write an attention-grabbing headline (subject), and click Publish. You just wrote your first blog.

One of the greatest benefits of this exercise is the amount of cutting-edge information about your topic that you will be learning on a daily basis as you read the five blog posts. By the end of the week, you will have read 25 different blog posts. As your brain begins to process the new information, you will begin to come up with your own ideas based on your interpretation of the blogs that you read. Keeping in mind that the blogs you are reading are all within the niche that you are interested in, you will quickly come up with exciting new content that will appeal to your readers.

Building Blog Traffic

The fastest way to build blog traffic is through social media websites such as Facebook and Twitter. Posting links to your high-quality content will attract the right kind of potential business partners and customers to your blog.

When you work with a design team like Wordpress Makeover, they will set you up with an opt-in box in the side panel of your blog. This feature will allow you to begin capturing some of your readers' information by offering a free report or something else of value in return for their name and e-mail address.

Once you begin to build a list using an autoresponder like iContact or AWeber, you can utilize a traffic driving strategy that will begin to move your blog up the traffic rankings online at a fast pace. The strategy is very simple.

First, you write a high-quality blog post. Then you take the link and post it on social media websites such as Facebook and Twitter. Next you send an e-mail to your opt-in list, letting them know about your new blog post.

This strategy has been proved to create blog traffic much more quickly than relying on search engines alone.

Blogging can be a great long-term strategy and one that I recommend to everyone, but to achieve payoff, it takes some time, commitment, and patience.

One network marketing leader who has come on the scene and really taken advantage of blogging as a method to build a network marketing business is Ray Higdon. Ray went from personal foreclosure to Fiji in 24 months. After losing millions in real estate and being completely devastated, Ray rose from the ashes to become the number-one income earner in his network marketing company as well as a top online marketer. His message is that anyone can accomplish anything regardless of his or her current circumstances. Ray has been featured on many of our industries top stages and publications and loves helping others with his training. Ray was born in Indiana, has two boys (Brandon and Ethan), and loves showing them the life that network marketing can provide by traveling and making sure to have just as much fun as work. Ray is currently engaged to the love of his life, Jessica, and is set to be married in only two weeks from this writing; then they will be off to Fiji for a 10-day honeymoon. Ray provides daily tactics on lead generation, traffic, sponsoring and recruiting, and all things network marketing on his blog at www.RayHigdon.com.

I had a chance to sit down with Ray and ask him about his success:

Ty Tribble: You are retired from your traditional job and work your business full time. What does your daily schedule look like?

Ray Higdon: Honestly, I work fairly hard Monday through Wednesday. I create one to two pieces of content, study something for self-improvement for at least an hour, and typically have some coaching calls I take care of. I do try to book at least one "thing" each night for my business Monday through Wednesday. This could be a webinar, conference call, or a meeting. Thursday through Sunday I just don't work a whole lot unless I am traveling for my team.

Ty Tribble: How do you get going when you don't feel like "doing it"?

Ray Higdon: I am a pretty logical dude who is freakishly disciplined. If I do not create a piece of content almost every day, I get nervous jitters. I have a set routine that gets completed every day unless I am traveling. I evaluate when I don't feel like doing something, and if it is going to greatly impact my business or is part of my routine, I just do it.

Ty Tribble: What is (was) your biggest fear?

Ray Higdon: It used to be public speaking, but I definitely worked past that. Now I would say my biggest fear is that I ever lose a handle on why I do my business. I have seen others go through this, and they start to despise the industry that treated them so well. I believe my awareness of that fact will prevent it from every happening.

Ty Tribble: When you get several nos in a row, what do you do?

Ray Higdon: Well, when I started my business, I was in personal foreclosure and my girlfriend was working at a makeup counter to pay our utility bills. I had to get nos. I actually had a "no goal" of 20 nos per day. I am simply not addicted to any outcome, so nos do not faze me at all. I think daily meditation has helped with this too.

Ty Tribble: What is your online strategy, and where does blogging fit in?

Ray Higdon: Blogging is my main strategy for providing value to the marketplace, getting leads, and creating content. My blog is ranked 16,000 worldwide and 4,000 in the United States for traffic, and that means I get 1.2 to 1.6 million hits per month to my blog. It sure didn't happen overnight, and for a technically challenged dude like me, it wasn't easy, but it has been worth it. I typically generate around 30 leads per day on autopilot from my blog.

Ty Tribble: Tell us about your offline strategy.

Ray Higdon: I still do house meetings, although not as many as I used to, and I do hotel meetings. I love to attend large marketing functions, get business cards, and then follow up with leads. Offline is the most duplicating way to build a business, so I certainly embrace doing and teaching it as well as the online strategies.

14

E-Mail Marketing and
Selling with Words

"THE MONEY IS in your list." This statement, often tossed around by Internet marketers, is only partially true. The actual money is in the relationship that you have with your e-mail list. Before we dig into the art and science of e-mail marketing, let's cover some list-building basics.

First, you will need an e-mail marketing company to help you manage your list and allow you to schedule autoresponders and timed e-mails. AWeber, iContact, and GetResponse are probably the most trusted and most popular e-mail autoresponders. I personally use iContact, but have many high-earning friends who use AWeber and GetResponse. These companies will help you manage your e-mail campaigns.

You build your list by offering something of value, such as a free ebook, special report, or video series in exchange for a prospect's contact information. The more information you ask for, such as name, e-mail address, and phone number, the fewer the number of people who will fill out your form, but the lead will actually be more qualified. Asking for less information, such as just the prospects e-mail address, will likely get you more opt-ins, but they will be less likely to respond to future offers.

There are multiple ways to get people to sign up for your list, such as:

- **Lead Capture or Squeeze Page:** A lead capture page or squeeze page is a web page that entices the reader to enter his or her contact information in exchange for something of value. These pages usually consist of a headline followed by a subheadline, some bullet points or a paragraph with a closing call to action, and of course your e-mail opt-in form.
- **Video Lead Capture Page:** A video capture page is similar to squeeze page or lead capture page, with the exception

being that the written content is replaced by a video. The conversion rates for traditional lead capture pages or squeeze pages versus a video lead capture page has changed many times over the years. The best way to see which one works best for you is to test them.

- **Blog Opt-In:** A blog or sidebar opt-in form is best described as a mini-lead capture page that is embedded in the side panel of a blog. Obviously, you will be limited in the number of words you use, but the sidebar opt-in is a valuable way to build your list, especially once you begin to get a reasonable amount of traffic.

- **Website Contact Form:** This would be similar to the blog opt-in, except it's really more of a Contact Me type of form. You can still use this to build your list, but you will also be able to answer specific questions for people and relate more directly to those who might want to contact you.

- **Pop-ups:** Pop-ups tend to be very controversial, with a lot of people having extreme reactions to them; however, when done correctly, a pop-up is a great way to add people to your list. The key to success when it comes to a pop-up is to ensure that the pop-up directly relates to the content on your site and is value-driven, as opposed to a big sales pitch.

Most people struggle with the technical side of creating these types of opt-ins, pages, and pop-ups, so I recommend checking out the following resources that offer simple, step-by-step templates and tools to help you along the way.

Lead Capture or Squeeze Pages and Video Capture Pages

- iLeadSystem
- MyLeadSystemPro
- OptimizePress

PopUp Domination is my preferred tool for adding pop-ups on my blogs and other pages. It's a pretty simple and straight-forward WordPress plug-in.

One of the most amazing benefits of e-mail marketing is the leverage it provides. Leverage is a great benefit of blogging as well, and they work hand in hand.

Picture yourself doing a presentation in front of 10 people in a living room. You can have a pretty big impact on 10 people. Now think of yourself conducting the same meeting in front of 1,000 people at a large hotel. More people always equal a greater impact. How about 10,000 people at a large convention?

What if you got crazy and held an event with 93,000 people at the Los Angeles Memorial Coliseum? Think about the logistics of putting on an event with more than 90,000 attendees, but also think about the potential impact you could make if you had the chance to communicate with the crowd, even if it was only for five minutes.

What would you say about your business?

Okay, leave the daydream for a moment and come back to reality. What if I told you that people today are communicating with 100,000 or more people on a regular basis by leveraging e-mail technology?

If you build your list, you can have 100, 1,000, 10,000, and even 100,000 or more people listening to your message.

You know that five-minute speech you were going to make to the 93,000 people at the Los Angeles Memorial Coliseum? Well, you can actually create a five-minute video and send it out to your list with the push of a button.

But there is a true art to communicating with an e-mail list, and I believe the art is rooted in our ability to emotionally connect with the reader through our writing.

Emotionally connecting with your readers always revolves around stories, and these stories will separate your e-mails from the competitions' in a big way. Few marketers understand the value of connecting their e-mails together in a story format. They typically go from one promotion to the next promotion with very little connection to the emotional connection that was made in the initial capture page.

Your story will be spread out over a series of e-mails where you will build trust and an emotional bond with your reader. The good news is that these e-mails can be written in advance. You do the work once (with occasional updates and tweaks), and the e-mail sequence has the ability to pay you time and time again.

Remember, the main purpose of your autoresponder e-mail sequence is to establish a real relationship by making a meaningful connection. In Chapter 13, we talked about reading other blogs within your niche on a regular basis. I suggested reading five blog posts each day. If you follow my suggestion, you will have read more than 100 blog posts in a month even if you are taking the weekends off.

As you study other blogs, you will absolutely find valuable bits of information that you will be able to share with your readers over time and perhaps within the context of your story.

Creating an emotional connection with your readers has the potential to pay off very big in the long run. You are working to relate to your readers, building relationships and suggesting that you are "one of them," but you can also begin to get a clear gauge on what exactly your readers are looking for.

Once you figure out what your readers are looking for, you give it to them! Give the readers what they want in the form of valuable content and offers, and they will respond by purchasing your products and becoming your business partners in the future.

I found people relate most to the e-mails that I send that carry my own personal voice and style. Stories are always best, but even when I am in sales mode, my readers respond best when I am conversational.

Once you have established a solid relationship with your readers, do not be afraid to sell. Many people are afraid of sales, but true sales is providing something that people need or solving a problem. If I am dying for a cup of coffee and I see a latte stand on a street corner, do you think I want them to sell me a cup of coffee? Of course I want the cup of coffee, and I might even be willing to pay extra money for it under the right circumstances.

Another great way to connect with your readers is to create short videos on a subject that they are interested in. I like to post the video on my blog and then send my e-mail subscribers to the blog post that contains the video. Between conversational e-mails and the occasional video, you will be surprised at how well people feel like they know you, even though you have never met in person.

Last, one of the greatest strategies I learned was to get my readers in the habit of clicking on a link in every e-mail. Usually I would include the link toward the bottom of the e-mail. I might include a bonus video and five secrets related to the topic, or I might even include a link to a separate article or website that contains more valuable content. Getting your reader in the habit of clicking on a link in every e-mail will pay great dividends when you want them to click on a link to buy something.

15

Video Marketing

Your Own Virtual TV Station

VIDEOS ARE A great way to build trust and influence on a mass scale. People who watch videos on a blog or through an e-mail list often feel like they know the creator of the video because they have enjoyed the value and the time spent together. The other wonderful advantage of creating videos is their inherent ability to rank highly in search engines. A little known fact is that YouTube is actually the second largest search engine online, with Google holding the number one spot.

Google actually owns YouTube, so there might be some correlation between ranking highly on YouTube and ranking highly on Google. YouTube is currently ranked third in overall web traffic after Google and Facebook, and it is only one of many video sites online. YouTube is far and away the top video website, with an estimated 450 million monthly unique visitors, but other highly ranked video sites include Hulu, DailyMotion, Metacafe, MegaVideo, MySpace Video, Yahoo! Video, and Vimeo.

In addition to generating search engine traffic and building trust, there are a lot of other great reasons to consider using videos as part of your online marketing strategy:

- **Creating a video is relatively easy.** The level of technical know-how needed to create and upload a video to your YouTube account is not genius level. If you are lost, simply go to YouTube and search for "How to upload a video to YouTube."
- **Video marketing is inexpensive.** Many people already have a video camera, and if they don't have a video camera, many have cell phones that include a video camera. I see a lot of people waste time and energy being overly concerned about video quality, and in most circumstances, the quality is not really all that important. However, there are

159

obvious things to consider regarding video quality, such as not trying to record a video while standing next to an airport or while in a windstorm.

■ **Video subject and tags (or keywords) can be highly targeted.** Keywords, tags, and the title of your videos are used to index the videos on YouTube and other sites, so you are free to create a video and target it toward your exact niche market. The more you target your video to a specific niche, the better.

■ **Videos don't have to take a lot of time to film and produce.** In many cases, a five-minute video can be edited and uploaded onto a video site or blog in 30 minutes or less. Many experts even suggest keeping your videos between two and four minutes. Attention spans are not what they used to be, and people will really enjoy grabbing a great nugget of information and content in a short time period.

Creating a Powerful Video

Here are a few tips to help you create a powerful video:

■ **Keep it simple.** A short, plainspoken video with a powerful strategy or piece of content is perfect, especially when you are getting started.

■ **Spend some time brainstorming.** Coming up with the title of a video before the video is actually created is a good way to make sure that you are covering all bases when it comes to utilizing keywords in the title, description, and tags. You can use Google's keyword tool to find keywords that apply to the overall video concept that you have in mind. Remember that stuffing a bunch of keywords into the title, description, and tags of a video that don't really apply to the content is a surefire way to alienate people from your future videos. Your headline or title will really sell the video, so make sure you spend some extra time coming up with a powerful headline. A good formula for creating a headline is to incorporate "how to" with your specific keyword phrase and a phrase that builds curiosity and intrigue, for example, "How to Create an MLM Marketing Blog—Secret Footage." I spent some time going into keyword research in Chapter 12, but one important thing to consider is that it will be very difficult to land on the front page of Google for "MLM"; however, landing on the front page of Google for what is called a long-tail keyword, such as "MLM Marketing," is much easier. Have fun with your keywords and titles and see what works best for you. Next you will need to work on your video description. The first thing you want to do is post your URL in the video description. This could be a URL to a lead capture page or to a Facebook page. After you insert your URL, you will want to include your main keyword phrases. An example of a description might look like this: "http://tytribble.com—Visit my MLM Marketing Blog to download my '5 Crazy MLM Marketing Strategies.' MLM Marketing Strategy #4 will tell you how to create an impossible-to-ignore MLM Marketing Video." Last, make sure you fill out the tags section with a handful of keywords that relate to your video.

■ **Use an outline.** Outlining the key points of what you want to cover in your video is the best way to give your video a natural feel while keeping you on track with the main points you want to cover. Most of the time, reading from a word-for-word script is easy to spot, inauthentic, and awkward.

■ **Be yourself.** If you are generally a shy person, it's really okay to come across as a bit shy on your videos. Your video has the opportunity to be exposed to a lot of people at a viral level online, and chances are many people who watch your video will have similar shy feelings just like you. People will relate to you because you are authentic and because you are being you.

- **Look directly into the camera and smile.** When I suggest that you "be you," I am really suggesting that you be a happy and excited (not scary excited) but genuinely enthusiastic you. One of the mistakes people make most often is they forget to smile.
- **Use the first 15 to 20 seconds on the video to sell the rest of the video.** We live in an ADD (attention deficit disorder) society today, and it is very easy to click off of a video. Make sure that you take the first 15 to 20 seconds of the video and enthusiastically sell people on the benefits of what they are going to get if they stick around to watch the next five minutes of the video.
- **Use a call to action.** I have seen a lot of videos where people do everything right. Great lighting, great content, the person is personable and genuine . . . and then we get to the end of the video, where it ends with a big, fat thud. No invitation to act or call to action. If you are not selling something specifically in the video, I suggest sending them to your e-mail list opt-in or to your Facebook fan page to Twitter. Think about some way to connect with the video viewers. You never know who is watching the video, and you don't want to let them get away. A simple call to action example would be, "Click the link below so that we can connect up on Facebook. I often post bonus content on my Facebook page, so use the Like button to avoid missing out on any cool bonus material."

Marketing Your Video

There is no secret that YouTube is the obvious choice for your videos, but as mentioned earlier, there are a lot of other video sites that will bring you traffic. The problem many people face is finding the time to upload a video to all of these sites. That's where a video submission tool comes in handy. Most of the video marketers that I know use Traffic Geyser, which is a paid service to send out their videos all across the Internet. Traffic Geyser has a 30-day trial, so you can do a good job of testing the tool before you commit to using it for the long term. Tube Mogul is a free service that you might want to consider if you are on a budget.

After your video is posted online, it is now time to market it. Here are some suggestions that will increase the traffic to your video:

- **Find high-ranking videos with lots of views on your topic and make your video a response.** This strategy is very easy, and it can pay off in a huge way. The trick is to find a video that has a lot of views but relates specifically to your video. Next, click on "post a video response," then choose your video. As long as the person with the high-traffic video has enabled the "post a video response" option, your video will show up under the high-traffic video almost immediately.
- **Tweet about your video on Twitter.**
- **Post a link to your video on Facebook.** For increased exposure, you might want to create an event around the launch of your video. You set up the day and time of your video launch and invite your friends. Make sure that your video contains valuable content that is applicable to the friends you invite.

- **Use your e-mail list to send out a link to your video.** Again, make sure that the video applies to the list you choose. You will gain status and influence in your niche market if you continually provide content that people are truly looking for versus continuous product pitches.
- **Post your video on your blog.** This is pretty much a no-brainer, but I am often surprised at how many video marketers completely ignore the power of blogging.

Video is estimated to account for 64 percent of all online traffic by the year 2014, according to Cisco.[1] And I can tell you that the most successful online network marketers today are all using video content within their current strategy.

---

[1] www.reelseo.com/cisco-video-online-major-source-traffic-2014/

16

Utilizing Social Media

THE IMPACT OF social media sites like Twitter, Facebook, and LinkedIn has been enormous on the network marketing industry. YouTube can also be considered a social media site, and we covered it in Chapter 15.

Most people belong to one or more of these social media sites, but few people grasp the power of using the sites for business. Of course, there are some people who seem to grasp the power, but only in terms of spamming their friends with link after link and pitch after pitch.

If you are brand-new to the idea of using social media, I recommend that you start with Facebook and spend the vast majority of your social media time learning the ins and outs of the site. The traffic on Facebook is astounding.

Here are some Facebook statistics:

- Facebook has more than 800 million active users, and on any given day, 50 percent of them log in.
- There are more than 900 million pages, groups, and events, and the average user is connected to 80 of them.
- An impressive 250 million pictures are uploaded every day.
- Facebook users download applications more than 20 million times a day.

Twitter and LinkedIn are growing as well, but if you are just starting out, Facebook is a good place to spend the majority of your social media marketing time.

Let's begin with getting your Facebook site in order.

Personally, I use my main Facebook page for both business and personal connecting. These areas of my life overlap. Plus, I have fun doing what I do for a living, so I figure, why not keep them together. At the same time, I am always careful about blatantly pitching my business on my page; I am a lot more subtle. You never really know when a former high school classmate or friend from the past will be looking for an opportunity to earn more income.

Make sure that your bio is updated and that you have a nice profile picture uploaded. From a business perspective, the purpose behind your time spent on Facebook is to brand yourself and expend your influence in the community. I don't think you need a professional picture, but it should be a picture that shows your face—and you should be smiling. You want people to recognize you if you meet them on the street, so using an up-to-date picture is a good idea.

One thing that seems difficult for some people to understand is the friending process. When I speak at an event, I often hear some people say, "But I don't even know this person. Why would I want to be his friend?" Well the answer lies in the potential for a future business relationship. For business networking purposes, you want as many friends as possible, but at the same time, you don't want to overdo your outgoing friend requests.

To find people you might already know and people you might want to get to know, you can use the Friend Finder; alternatively, you might want to join a group or fan page that closely aligns with your product or business niche. Another great way to find people who you might align with is to look at friends of friends. I wouldn't add more than a handful of new friend requests each day because Facebook may look at it as spam-like behavior.

The most important thing to remember when making a friend request is to leave a personal message, something like, "Hi, Audrey. I see that we have a mutual friend in Carrie and we have a mutual interest in networking. I am looking to connect with people here on Facebook and would be honored if you would accept my friendship."

Adding new friends to your Facebook account should be an ongoing process until you reach about 4,900 friends. The Facebook limit is 5,000, but once you get close to the limit, you will no longer be able to Like things on the site. Yes, there is a downside to being popular! I found it easier to build a following on a personal page than it is to build a following on a fan page, but once you get to several thousand friends, it would be a good idea to consider a fan page.

My Facebook strategy is to post a mix of lifestyle and helpful content with the occasional offer sprinkled in (like 1 out of 10 posts). My lifestyle updates might include pictures of food, travel, and fun times with friends. It is very easy to see if one of your Facebook posts has struck a cord with your friends; all you have to do is count the number of comments you get. Surprisingly, one of the most commented posts I have ever had was a picture of a plate of food. For whatever reason, people love to see food on Facebook; travel pictures tend to attract just as much attention.

Think about taking pictures even if you are out and about (traveling) within your own town. For updates that do not relate directly to business but are more lifestyle focused, think about food, fun, travel, and friends.

When it comes to updates that are more business related, you want to be looked upon as a trusted advisor, so posting links to interesting articles and blog posts is a good way to move up the influence ladder.

Like blogging and other marketing online, success with social media has a lot to do with being consistent. Of course, sharing your own blog posts is a great way to expose people to your other valuable resources, such as your e-mail list.

Personally, I find my time spent on Facebook to be most rewarding, but LinkedIn is another option. Here are four tips to using LinkedIn to market your business.

1. LinkedIn can be great for search engine optimization. Be sure your profile is up to date and your website and blog links are active.
2. Set up your LinkedIn site to automatically update when you update your blog. This will keep your LinkedIn content fresh, even though you aren't actually visiting the site.
3. I have heard people are getting great results with LinkedIn advertising. Although the traffic is not as high as on Facebook, the demographic is significantly better when it comes to education and income.
4. Create a LinkedIn group centered on your niche and actively engage others who share the same interests.

Twitter is another site that might be worth your time, although it is even more important to really engage with people on Twitter. If you simply shoot out link after link to your Twitter followers, your results will not be good.

Other social media sites to consider having a look at include:

- Ning
- Google+
- Meetup
- Foursquare
- Yelp

Last, remember to use your time on social media sites wisely. There are a lot of things that you can get caught up in that waste valuable time—time you could be devoting to building your business. I try to keep my social media marketing to quick spurts of time throughout my day.

Conclusion

You have come to the conclusion of a book filled with techniques and strategies in addition to stories about people just like you who have doubled their income (or much more) with network marketing. I hope that you have caught glimpses of yourself in the success stories sprinkled throughout this book. The world is filled with people who have good intentions, but many of those people fail to act. They fail to implement what they learn because deep down, they wonder if they can really make it happen.

I am here to tell you that you can make it happen. I am no rock star or guru, and if you met me face to face, you would probably leave our meeting saying, "If Ty can do it, I'm gonna tear this up!"

John Wooden said, "Success comes from knowing that you did your best to become the best that you are capable of being." If you look through the interviews that I conducted for the book, you will find a theme that is pretty much universal.

Success in network marketing has very little to do with trying to accomplish something and a lot more to do with being the very best you that you can be. Please send me your feedback and success stories. I look forward to seeing what you accomplish.

You can contact me on Facebook at Facebook.com/TyTribble.fb or via my blog at TyTribble.com.

Index